Joy on
High Places

PEGGY MARGO WOJTOWICZ

DEDICATION

First and foremost, to my Lord, Who has given me the gift of this life and the faith to believe that, in His strength, I was capable of accomplishing this task. To my husband, Dan, for his unwavering love and support. To my daughter, Ashley, who inspires me by the powerful life she lives trusting God. To my son Aaron, for adding so much pure joy and sunshine to my life. I can't believe I get to be called "Mom" by the two of them.

CONTENTS

Preface

"If you want to change the world, pick up your pen and write."
- Martin Luther

ONE OF THE saddest sentences I know is, "I wish I had asked my mother or my father about that." I wish I had a nickel for every time I've heard a friend or family member or even myself repeat that sentence. As every parent knows, our children are not as interested in our fascinating lives as we are. It's normally only when they have children of their own – and feel the first twinges of their own advancing age – that they suddenly want to know more about their family heritage and lore. As William Zinsser states in *How to Write a Memoir*:

> "Writers are the custodians of memory, and that's what you must become if you want to leave some kind of record of your life and of the family you were born into. That record can take many shapes. It can be a formal memoir – a careful act of literary construction. Or it can be an informal family history, written to tell your

children and your grandchildren about the family they were born into. It can be the oral history that you extract by tape recorder from a parent or a grandparent too old or too sick to do any writing. Or it can be anything else you want it to be: some hybrid mixture of history and reminiscence. Whatever it is, it's an important kind of writing."

Too often memories die with their owner, and too often time surprises us by running out. I write this as a legacy to my children and grandchildren whose "souls dwell in the house of tomorrow, which [I] cannot visit, not even in [my] dreams" (Kahlil Gibran, "On Children"). I am the archer, my children the arrows. My duty is to release them and watch them fly. Part of preparing them to fly is intentionally connecting my children and grandchildren with the past to help them have a sense of identity. My actions echo into the next generation. According to an old African proverb, "When an old person dies, a library burns to the ground." This is my way of passing on part of our family library.

Remembering God's faithfulness in this memoir is also my way of giving thanks - of looking over my shoulder to see how His arms have carried me all the way. Why do I have spiritual Alzheimer's, always forgetting? How quickly I forget God's mercies. I empty of Truth and need to be refilled. I am so imperfect that I am ashamed to give any testimony, but then I realize it is exactly *because* of my imperfections that the glory goes to God, not to me. Revelation 12:11 says that the enemy is overcome "by the blood of the Lamb and the word of (our) testimony." I feel the need, yes even the compulsion, to put these things in writing for myself as well as those who read this and, like myself, are beset by chronic amnesia of the soul. My heart needs to express just a few of the amazing ways the Lord has led me. As I write, I ask God to give me the words that He wants me to say because, in the words of Ravi Zacharias, "Even fluency is a liability if one has nothing to say." Gratitude births trust and strengthens faith, and it is my hope that remembering God's help in the past will cause those who read this to truly believe and trust Him for the future.

God very clearly charged me to live my life as a living testimony of His grace as I faced the crushing circumstances I experienced in 1994. Going through Stage III breast cancer with surgery, chemotherapy, radiation and facing an 80% likelihood of not surviving, left me one night telling God that I would prefer to be with Him than to stay and endure all of that only to die anyway. I truly longed to be with Him and wasn't afraid to die. My early demise would have been devastating for my family and friends but looked like sweet relief to me.

Although my husband, Dan, was unaware of these thoughts, shortly after I spoke those words to God, Dan walked into the room with a Scripture he said he knew was intended for me. It was the story of Jesus healing the man with many demons, found in Mark 5. In Mark 5:18 the healed man, "begged [Jesus] that he might be with Him. However, Jesus did not permit him, but said to him, 'Go home to your friends and tell them what great things the Lord has done for you, and how He has had compassion on you.'" For me, that was a defining moment. Those words impacted me in a powerful way and energized me to endure the long months of suffering and uncertainty ahead. "Stay and be a testimony of my compassion, power, authority, and Lordship." That is what I felt the Lord was saying to me that day, and I've lived the rest of my life in the shadow of those words. His faithfulness has compelled me to be vulnerable enough to put my praise of Him down in ink.

Amy Carmichael, one of my favorite authors, was a missionary to orphans in India in the 1920s. She rescued hundreds of orphaned children, especially little girls that would be dedicated to Hindu gods for use in sexual temple rituals. In 1931 she prayed, "God please do with me whatever you want. Do anything that will help me to serve You better." That same day, she fell, suffering fractures that crippled her for the rest of her life.

Rather than respond with discouragement or bitterness toward God for her situation, Amy Carmichael embraced this opportunity to demonstrate God's faithfulness before a much larger "host" of witnesses. Amy stayed in her weakness. She shared her weakness and let those she had come to serve, serve her. Though she was bedridden for the remainder of her life, Amy's beloved "children" had the freedom to enter her bedroom and share their hearts with their beloved "mother." Now Amy had the quiet times that allowed her to write books, poems, and letters that were translated and shared around the world. God used Amy Carmichael's story in my decision to write this memoir.

Health brings a freedom very few realize until they no longer have it. Two years ago, I started to experience chronic pain and limited mobility due to back problems. I struggled to wrap my head around the fact that my future might hold worsening pain and even crippling immobility. One day as I knelt and prayed, the Lord reminded me that even if I wound up bedridden, I could still glorify Him with my thoughts, prayers, attitude, and words. I sensed that He was asking me if I would continue to praise Him regardless of what He allowed. I said I would.

As I prayed and looked at Scripture with my Bible open, out fell the sheet with the above story about Amy Carmichael's struggles. I had been contemplating writing this memoir for a long time. I told the Lord that if I became immobile, I would write for Him. I sensed He was asking me if I would write for Him even if I was *not* immobile. I said I would, and, by His grace, I have kept my word. It's one thing to write when that's physically the only thing one can do. It's quite another thing again to have the discipline to sit down and write when you have complete mobility and your days get filled with the business of life. Thankfully, my back pain is manageable, and I have complete mobility, which has made it a wrestling match with my will to allow sufficient time in my days to finish what I started.

I thank God for the grace to respond to my chronic back problems not with anger and bitterness toward Him but as a challenge to use this time to write for His glory. All truth is God's truth. The words that follow are the truth, as best I can remember, as God has written His truth into my life and has allowed me the privilege of sharing all that He has done.

CHAPTER 1

My True Confession

> *"Oh God, I have tasted of Your goodness, and it has both satisfied me and made me thirsty for more."*
> ~ A.W. Tozer

THE DAY BEFORE EASTER, Saturday, April 13, 1963, dawned warm and sunny. It was springtime in The Heights, my neighborhood in Wilkes-Barre, Pennsylvania. I was ten years old, and my best friends, Maryann, Joyce, and I were on our way to St. Joseph's Catholic Church to go to confession so we could receive communion the next day. Easter was the one day of the year I was sure to attend church, and the day before Easter was the only day of the year I went to confession. If going to Sunday Mass was sure to cause a nervous knot in my stomach, going to confession was the epitome of the dreaded Catholic experience magnified by the fact that I only confessed once a year. Other "good" Catholics had just a few sins to list since they confessed often enough not to amass a huge number. I had an entire year of stored-up sins which needed to be confessed in one sitting – or should I say, one kneeling. It's like going to the dentist: the more you put it off the worse it is when you finally go. My dentist has a sign on the ceiling above my dental chair that reads, "Ignore your teeth and they'll go away." Today I wished that were true of my unconfessed sins.

Waiting in line, I watched the red light over the door of the confessional to see when it was my turn to enter. Soon the light changed to green, signaling for me to go. I entered the dark, quiet confessional booth and knelt to wait. With the priest seated between two penitents, muffled voices assured me that the priest was hearing the confession of the person on the other side of the booth. My heart pounded loudly. In my young life, this was one of the most dreaded days of the year: the day I received penance. Church made me nervous; but then again, at this point in my life, everything made me nervous.

Suddenly, the solid partition which covered the screen separating us slid open. This was my cue to begin.

"Bless me, Father, for I have sinned," I said. "It has been one year since my last confession."

At the tender age of ten years old, my grasp of the Ten Commandments was a little shaky. I guess I wasn't listening too well in catechism classes because somewhere along the line I acquired the mistaken impression that "thou shalt not commit adultery" meant "thou shalt not act like an adult." I cringed, but I had to spill the beans. Finally, I blurted out, "I have committed adultery 100 times."

Dead silence. At this point, the priest normally would start handing out my penance. Not this time. The stunned silence on his part was deafening. *What's wrong with this guy?* I wondered. I was further confused when he asked how old I was.

"Ten years old, father." More stunned silence.

"Are you married?" he asked.

Now I was the one who was stunned. "No!" was my indignant reply. What was wrong with this guy, anyway? In what universe does a ten year old get married? And why wasn't he just handing out "Hail Mary's" and "Our Fathers" like any self-respecting priest would do?

It was then that he asked, "My child, what do you think adultery means?"

After I explained my definition, it was the only time in my life I detected a muffled chuckle coming from the dreaded priest.

Thank God, he didn't tell me what adultery really meant. That was saved for the trip home when I nonchalantly asked my girlfriends the definition of adultery. I stopped cold in my tracks when they told me. The poor guy. I was certain that for years to come he had a high old time telling that story to his clerical-collared friends.

By God's grace I never experienced marital adultery, yet I write this testimony as a confession of sorts, a confession that I am indeed the adulterous woman, guilty of spiritual adultery against God. How often have I put my trust in the things this world has to offer – money, relationships, health, and security – instead of God?

But the Lord has faithfully pursued me and drawn me back. "You adulterous people, don't you know that friendship with the world means enmity against God? Therefore, anyone who chooses to be a friend of the world becomes an enemy of God." (James 4:4) My story is not about who I am. It is about Whose I am. My testimony is one of my great faithlessness and His great faithfulness. I set out to write this memoir as praise to my God and Savior, the Lord Jesus Christ, and His incredible faithfulness to my family and me. The Ancient of Days pursued me with His love, and I will spend all eternity praising Him for that.

CHAPTER 2

Dan, Dan the Guitar Man

"It is the LORD who goes before you, He will be with you, He will not leave you or forsake you, do not fear or be dismayed."
- Deuteronomy 31:8

I WAS A mere 16 years old when my best friend, Janice, became acquainted with a young man named Danny Wojtowicz. Janice had a serious boyfriend, Jimmy, so I knew Danny's interest in Janice was purely platonic. I was aware of Danny and his twin, Dave. They were one year ahead of me in high school, and I always thought Danny was cute. As Janice and Danny's friendship progressed, I became intrigued by the things she said about him. "Danny's so silly, he doesn't want me to walk in the rain so he brought me an umbrella," or "Danny insists on giving me a ride home, so I don't have to walk." I was impressed with the thoughtfulness of this young man. After a while, I mentioned to Janice that if Danny happened to ask me to go out, I wouldn't say no. She got the point and passed that tidbit along to him.

It was May of 1969 when Danny asked me out, and our first date was a double date to a drive-in movie with Janice and Jimmy. I was thoroughly smitten by this clean cut, hard working young man who had the most wonderful sense of humor. Danny played guitar and had "gigs" most weekends but always held another job during the week. Soon, we were inseparable. When his band, The Projected Image, played at a dance, I was there. When I cheered at a football or basketball game, he was there. Danny came to my house to help his little cheerleader make banners for the pep rally or to hang in the football players' locker room before a big game. When I finished cheering at football games on bitter cold Northeastern Pennsylvania evenings, Danny was there to pick me up in his 1955 International truck with the heater blasting, a blanket on the seat, and a cup of piping hot chocolate waiting for me. I took note of, and was duly impressed by, the fact that Danny cleaned the house for his mother and in general treated her like gold.

Five years later when Dan (as he now chose to be called) graduated from Penn State, he was offered a position as a mechanical draftsman with The DuPont Company in Wilmington, Delaware. I thought my heart would break when he moved two and a half hours away. To us, it might as well have been the other side of the country. Dan made the drive home every weekend to see me and spent a good deal of his pay check on long distance phone calls. We couldn't bear to be apart so, just six months after Dan started working for DuPont, we were married on January 5, 1974. After our honeymoon in the Poconos we moved to Newark, Delaware. In June of 1985, we moved to Aiken, SC where Dan worked first for DuPont and then for Bechtel at the Savannah River Site.

Dan and I have witnessed a lot of life and, in some ways, grew up together. It's wonderful to have someone who shares my high school memories and came from the same home town. I thank God for giving me a mate who has walked faithfully beside me through all that life sent our way for over 40 years. We held hands on the sofa and watched the first man walk on the moon in 1969. We dated through the turmoil of the Vietnam era. I held my breath when Dan was almost drafted for active duty but was turned down for medical reasons. After twelve years of marriage in 1985, we leaned on each other when we made the decision to move to the South. Dan never left my side when I gave birth to our children. We've stood side by side as we've endured several moves, sickness, the death of our parents and a sibling, challenging careers, raising children, and all that life can hurl at a family.

CHAPTER 3

From Fear to Faith

"Then beware, lest you forget the Lord, Who brought you out of the land of Egypt, from the house of bondage."
- Deuteronomy 6:12

NOVEMBER 1977

I WAS 24 years old and had struggled with fear and anxiety all my life. Although today I have an inner serenity and strength, those things did not come naturally for me. They are the product of many hours of time spent with God. Error and false thinking had me in bondage; the truth set me free. I had an aching need in my life and the inability to fill that need with anything other than the peace of God. My anxieties were so out of control that I was barely able to function. I quit my job due to panic attacks and even became fearful of leaving my home. I soon became unable to drive or go shopping. My thoughts were rambling, frightening, and seemed out of my control. I leaned toward obsessive-compulsive tendencies such as repeatedly washing my hands, touching things a certain number of times, and incessantly checking locks on doors. The term agoraphobia was not one I was familiar with nor would it become a household word for many years. I suffered to one degree or another with this paralyzing, life-choking anxiety for almost seven years from the ages of 17 to 24. Suffice it to say I was miserable and desperate.

Even though I had grown up in the Catholic Church, God had little impact on my daily life. I was your typical Christmas-and-Easter church attendee. I saw no need for God or prayer. As a matter of fact, my idea of prayer wasn't opening my heart to God, but rather the idle rote prayers that I found meaningless but recited when I attended Mass. However, out of sheer desperation I started to simply talk to God. I found myself asking often and fervently for God to heal me of my fears. I didn't know where else to turn. And so I had become a seeker. But the Bible clearly states that if anyone finds themselves seeking after the things of God, it is because God is first drawing them. "None is righteous, no not one. No one understands; no one seeks for God." (Romans 3:10) It is God seeking us, as John 6:44 clearly states: "No one can come to Me unless the Father who sent me draws him." I wanted deliverance from my fears, but what I found out was the source of that deliverance was from an intimate relationship with Jesus Christ.

A friend knew about my anxieties and shared with me *The Power of Positive Thinking* by Norman Vincent Peale. Normally I would have thought this was a simplistic, trite, and even silly book to be dismissed, but I was desperate, so I read it. The only thing I can say is that it was the first time in my life I ever heard anybody talking about Jesus Christ like He was still alive. Last I'd seen of Him, He was dead and hanging on a cross. Talking to Him like He was alive and learning He was someone I could have a relationship with was a novel idea to me.

The book was filled with verses like "I can do all things through Christ Who strengthens me" (Philippians 4:13) and "God has not given you a spirit of fear, but of power, and of love and of a sound mind" (2 Timothy 1:7). Peale said that, just like nature, our minds abhor a vacuum. They are always occupied by something, and we can choose that something. In order to get rid of unwanted thoughts we have to replace them with positive thoughts. The positive thoughts he used were Scriptures. Even though I had never read a Bible in my life, and had previously found it dry and boring when I glanced through one, I began to devour the Scriptures he quoted and to cling to them when in challenging situations. These verses seemed to be the only positive things in my life.

I was learning that our lives flow out of what we think, and the Word of God is the most powerful tool in transforming our thinking. The battle for the mind is a spiritual battle. As Romans 12:2 puts it, "Don't copy the behavior and customs of this world, but let God transform you into a new person by changing the way you think. Then you will learn to know God's will for you, which is good and pleasing and perfect." I was beginning to see that my mind is a battlefield. For the first time in my life, joy began to creep in as God gave me new weapons for the battle.

In his book, Peale clearly states that Christ's sacrificial death paid for my sin, and receiving that fact to be true by faith is what brings us into a relationship with Christ. John 3:16 was new to me: "For God so loved the world that He gave His one and only Son, that whoever believes in Him shall not perish but have eternal life." Peale stated we could know we were going to heaven, a novel idea for any Catholic. Salvation was by grace through faith, not my works. This was good news to my struggling and exhausted soul.

These new truths I was discovering began to have a visible, practical effect on my life. In 1977, Dan and I became involved in the Amway business. One evening in November of that year Dan and I were at an Amway conference. As was my habit, we sat in the back near the door so I could escape if I had a panic attack. I would retreat to the car and wait there for Dan. I began to hyperventilate and felt dizzy and anxious and told Dan I was going out to the car. He knew the drill. As I sat in the car, I was utterly at the end of myself. I cried and told God that I quit trying to do this myself. I didn't know how to help myself, but that He needed to do for me what I couldn't do for myself. I had heard that I needed to confess my sins and ask forgiveness, and He would be my burden bearer. I had to repent of trying to earn my own salvation. Romans 4:5 declares, "But people are counted as righteous, not because of their work, but because of their faith in God who forgives sinners." I laid it all on Him.

After I prayed, I felt an indescribable peace like I'd never experienced before. I not only felt better physically and emotionally, but I felt like the burdens of the world had been instantly lifted off my shoulders. Normally when I would retreat like this, it was days before I recovered physically and emotionally. This was instantaneous, physical, emotional and, most importantly, spiritual. I was ecstatic! I had energy and a new serenity. I didn't know the Christian lingo, so I had no words to describe what happened; all I knew was that I felt great.

Dan was surprised when I uncharacteristically came back into the meeting. I don't remember trying to even explain to him what happened because I wasn't sure myself. I only knew that something was different. What happens when anyone has their eyes opened by God? This is the miracle. There was a moment when Christ was irrelevant to me. One day, He was not compelling. Other things held my affections and guided my life: friends, work, recreation. But now, suddenly, Christ was irresistibly attractive and all-compelling. This is the miracle that God shines into our hearts, to give sight to the glory of Christ. "For God, who said, 'Let there be light in the darkness,' has made this light shine in our hearts so we could know the glory of God that is seen in the face of Jesus Christ." (2 Corinthians 4:6)

Since that moment, I have never been the same again. This is a mighty and unmistakable work of the Holy Spirit accomplished in every single believer who declares that Jesus Christ is Lord. 1 Corinthians 12:3 says, "Therefore, I want you to understand that no one speaking in the Spirit of God ever says 'Jesus is accursed' and no one can say 'Jesus is Lord' except in the Holy Spirit." According to 2 Corinthians 5:17,

"Anyone who belongs to Christ has become a new person. The old life is gone; a new life has begun!" I was more than ready to give up my old life and bring on the new!

Don't misunderstand. I'm not saying that coming to Christ is a feeling. "If you confess with your mouth, 'Jesus is Lord,' and believe in your heart that God raised Him from the dead, you *will* be saved." (Romans 10:9) There is no mention of emotions there, just a promise that we can take to the bank. I have met many people who have come to faith in Christ and have felt nothing, but this was my experience.

A few weeks later, we went to a nondenominational worship service at an Amway rally. The speaker there talked about receiving Christ as Savior, and he gave an altar call. I felt like I was at a Billy Graham Crusade. I had always laughed at those crusades, but on this day it made sense, and I went down to the altar and publicly confirmed with God what I had already done in private in the car a few weeks earlier.

CHAPTER 4

Wrestling the Demon of Fear

"Worry is a demon sucking at the stream of your life."
~ George McDonald

"Both faith and fear may sail into your harbor,
but allow only faith to drop anchor."
~ Bear Grylls

SINCE I WAS unemployed because of my anxiety, I had all the time in
the world to read. I had a new, insatiable hunger for Scripture, and I
began to blow the dust off my Bible. I would sit up all night reading the
Bible, being amazed and feeling like I had been in a desert and now
found an unlimited water source. The missionary Hudson Taylor once
said, "I seem to have got to the edge only, but of a sea which is boundless;
to have sipped only, but of that which fully satisfies." Now I was having

the same experience. I couldn't get enough.

I soon found out that receiving Christ as my savior was just the beginning of being set free from my self-imposed prison. Through the Word of God, I began to see that I had what preacher Bob Harrington calls "stinkin' thinkin'." Although I was sure that no one else felt the same way I did, I found out that fear is common to all. It's not being afraid that is the issue. It's giving in to fear that limits us. I had given in to fear so many times as my world became smaller and smaller. Instead of experiencing less apprehension, limiting myself to a narrow world only increased my fears. I was allowing my emotions to dictate the choices I made. I would soon find out that God never designed emotions to think.

According to author Marilyn Meberg,

> "Emotions don't have brains. God gives us emotions to feel but brains to make choices with. We simply cannot count on our emotions. One day we wake up in a great mood and love everybody and the next day we wake up and everybody annoys us. We have been created with a will that is stronger than our emotions."

I found my freedom in this principle. We can choose to do something that goes against our feelings but is in our best interest. When I learned I could make a choice past my emotions that were not stable, then I began to find solid ground. Learning this process takes time. It is not natural to go against your own feelings. But when you have allowed your feelings to become so diseased that they are programming bizarre behavior, it takes time to conquer. I did this through the counsel of Scripture. "For God has not given us the spirit of fear, but of power, and of love, and of a sound mind" 2 Timothy 1:7. I realized that a lot of my thoughts came out of my own imbalance and mental process rather than out of the Truth of Scripture. A healthy mind takes hard work but what we gain from it is our greatest reward. My irrational fears gradually subsided as I renewed my mind with Truth instead of the lies I believed. Although my struggles didn't end instantly, within a few short months I was working again and living a joyful life.

Boy, can I relate to the following lyrics from "Free" by Ginny Owens: "Turning molehills into mountains, making big deals out of small ones, this is how it's been." That's one of my favorite songs because of the message. She goes on, "Till the day You pounded on my heart's door, and You shouted joyfully, 'You're not a slave anymore! You're free to dance. Forget about your two left feet.... I've given you My love and it's made you free!" Thank God, that's the story of my life. I hate that the beginning of my story is filled with fear and burdens and worries, but it's worth it all that the remainder of my life has been filled with God's love, joy, and a song on my lips and a dance in my step. If it took worry and tensions for God to get my attention, then bring it on! Fear is the sharp nail which has nailed me to Christ so that I could never want or dare to go on my own again. My life since those early days of agoraphobia is just a testimony to the deliverance and healing power of God that can happen in a life.

A full life, one spilling over with joy and peace, happens only when I come to trust the Great Lover of my soul. Fear keeps the life small. That's been a lesson I've had to learn over and over again on many different levels. I think we all do. Fear is the antithesis of trust. Often I find I don't want to muster the energy to trust. Trust requires intention, focus. Sadly, it seems easier to stress and worry. But isn't joy worth the effort of trust? I've found that the effort of trusting God and stepping out on faith is more than worth the exhilaration of watching Him work in and through me.

I've tried to be a student of those who are overcomers in spite of what seem like impossible situations. Michael J. Fox is one of those who seem to have a great attitude, regardless of physical limitations due to Parkinson's disease which will only worsen with time. When asked about his future, Fox wrote, "If you focus on the worst-case scenario, and it actually happens, you've lived it twice." Who wants to live their pain twice? It was the wise Corrie ten Boom who survived the Nazi concentration camp who said, "Worry does not empty tomorrow of its sorrow, it empties today of its strength." When you think of it, there is only one work God asks of us - believe. "Jesus told them, 'This is the only work God wants from you: Believe in the One He has sent" John 6:29, Living Translation.

The Bible is replete with the command, "Fear not." As I abandon myself to the Lord of the universe, He will give me rest. Matthew 11:28-30 says,

"Come to me, all you who are weary and burdened, and I will give you rest. Take my yoke upon you and learn from me, for I am gentle and humble in heart, and you will find rest for your souls. For my yoke is easy and my burden is light."

I have truly been liberated from bondage. I am no longer a slave to fear. I am a child of God. One of the most enduring joys of my life has been to share this good news with others and watch the Lord unlock the door of their self-imposed prison.

CHAPTER 5

Letting Scripture Lead

"My conscience is captive to the Word of God."
~ *Martin Luther*

"Since my eyes have looked on Jesus,
I've lost sight of all beside,
So enchained my spirit's vision,
Gazing on the Crucified"
~ *My Utmost for His Highest*

THE YEAR WAS 1980, three years since I had abandoned myself to God. I was overflowing with gratitude and love for this precious Father Who brought me peace like I'd never known. I had begun to go to Mass daily because it was the only avenue I had to worship the One I so badly wanted to worship. I also was veraciously reading and deeply reflecting on Scripture. An older friend and mentor taught me how to truly study God's Word for myself by looking at the entire Word of God. When I checked with the church we were attending to see if they offered a Bible study, the priest said they didn't but he gave me a book on the Catholic faith. In answer to my desire to know God's Word better, the priest also offered to meet with me for weekly discussion. I spent several months getting together with him as we discussed the teachings of the church in contrast to my understanding of Scripture. I tried in vain to reconcile Catholic doctrine with Scripture.

The more I studied, the more I also began to understand Hebrews chapters 9 and 10. These chapters would prove pivotal in my journey. Romans 6:23 declares, "For the wages of sin is death, but the free gift of God is eternal life in Christ Jesus our Lord." Hebrews 9:22 declares, "without the shedding of blood, there is no forgiveness of sins." The sacrifice of an animal, the first death, was the covering and payment for Adam's sin. Hebrews 9-10 and the book of Romans explain how Christ, the only truly perfect sacrifice, died once for all.

Once for all: that Scripture resounded in my heart and soul. I could no longer see Mass the same way as I came to understand that the Catholic Church performs the sacrifice at every Mass. Christ's work clearly was finished on the cross, once for my sin and the sin of mankind. The more I understood Scripture, the more I began to struggle with many of the church's doctrines. However, we continued for a short time to attend Mass even while questioning the church's traditions and practices. Although I know the Lord has his people inside as well as outside of the Catholic church, we soon found it necessary to attend a church which more closely aligns with Scripture.

Salvation by faith through grace was another area where I found Scripture to be clear. 2 Corinthians 5:19 says, "For God was in Christ, reconciling the world to himself, no longer counting people's sins against them. And He gave us this wonderful message of reconciliation." Verse 21 says, "For He made Him who knew no sin to be sin for us, that we might become the righteousness of God in Him."

Christ became our sin at the cross. He exchanged my sin for His righteousness. It is a finished work that we cannot earn but must receive as a free gift. He gives us the gift of Himself. Ephesians 2:8-9 states "For by grace you have been saved through faith. And this is not your own doing. It is the gift of God, not a result of works, so that no one may boast." Salvation is a gift we receive, not something we earn. Apart from Jesus Christ and his death on the cross, there is no salvation. As long as we truly rest in the finished work of Christ alone, the Bible teaches that we will be saved.

CHAPTER 6

The Dark Night of the Soul

"There's no one more thankful to sit at the table
than the one who best remembers hunger's pain"
~ from "Remember Your Chains"
by Steven Curtis Chapman

"It is doubtful whether God can bless a man greatly
until He has hurt him deeply."
~ A.W. Tozer

THERE ARE MANY references in Scripture to times of extreme testing which God sometimes allows in the lives of His children. Abraham experienced what Scripture describes in Genesis 15:12 as a "great darkness." Moses spent years on the back side of the wilderness. I'm not comparing myself with these great men of faith, but Scripture is replete with trials the Lord allows in the lives of believers to test their faith.

When the cancer diagnosis came in November 1994, and I was given only a 20% chance of survival, I knew I had an extremely difficult road ahead of me. It was a time I needed to lean on the Lord more than ever before. One afternoon I took a nap, and when I woke up I experienced what I can only describe as a sense of the absence of the presence of the Lord. It seemed like God had turned His back on me. I was inconsolable. This wasn't about cancer or fear, this was something different. It was a spiritual darkness that is impossible to adequately describe. I cried out to the Lord and told Him I wasn't sure I could get through this time in my life *with* Him, let alone *without* Him. I spent the day pacing the floor, praying and pretty much in spiritual and emotional agony.

As I lay in bed that night, I was unable to sleep and was still in emotional turmoil. It was then that my husband did for me one of the most precious things I've ever witnessed. Sensing my distress, my husband, the man God gave me as a life partner since age 16, quietly knelt down on the floor next to my side of the bed. Without saying a word, he took my hand and softly started to read Scripture to me. He read from the book of John. It calmed my soul in a way nothing else could. For the first time that day, I was able to truly relax and eventually fall asleep. But Dan didn't stop just because I was asleep. As I drifted in and out of a very fitful slumber, every time I woke up through the entire night he was there by my side, holding my hand and reading Scripture over me. Amazing! What a blessing of God to give me a loving husband who would lavish such a tender and self-sacrificing gift on me. It remains one of my fondest memories of Dan.

The next day I still had no feeling that the Lord was with me. I prayed Scripture from the book of Job: "Though He slay me, yet shall I praise Him." (Job 13:15) David often says in Psalms "yet shall I praise Him," and I continued to praise God based on truth rather than feeling. I told Him that I believed the truth of His Word when He said, "I will *never* leave you nor forsake you." (Deuteronomy 31:6) I had to trust that God would never leave me, even though my feelings told me just the opposite. It was a bare faith based on fact, not feelings.

That evening as I was on my knees in prayer, telling God I trusted His Word and knew He would never leave me in spite of feeling like He had, I suddenly had an awareness of His presence once again. It seemed like He had had his back turned toward me, and suddenly He turned to face me. I was ecstatic and praised Him joyfully! Ever since Adam and Eve, our focus tends to be toward ourselves instead of God. I don't ever fully see God for Who He is, but in those moments when I get a glimpse, I can hardly speak.

That experience undergirded me for the rest of my life. I realized that what I wanted more than healing, more than anything else in life was God Himself, not what He could give me or do for me, but just Him. It was not about whether I lived or died, because either way I had Him. I finally understood the verse in Psalm 73:25, "Whom have I in heaven but You? And there is none upon earth that I desire beside You. My flesh and my heart fail; but God is the strength of my heart and my portion forever."

God creates in each of us a craving for communion with Him. Unfortunately, we fill that craving with a million things and leave Him out. I learned from that experience that my trust had to be based on truth and not feelings, and that God and God alone is what my soul desires. And I know that I know that I know that Jesus Christ is Lord and the Only Way to the Father. I have put all my eggs in that basket, and I will live and die by it, period. If I am wrong, then I am to be pitied. "And if our hope in Christ is only for this life, we are more to be pitied than anyone in the world." (1 Corinthians 15:19)

Jesus Himself said He is the Way, the Truth, and the Life. No man comes to the Father but by Him. (John 14:6) He claimed to be God in the flesh. Jesus was a real, historical figure whom everyone recognizes to have truly existed. In order for Jesus to make that claim, He either had to be an insane maniac or God in the flesh. There are no other choices. When trying to research and disprove the deity of Christ, Tom Skinner said, "I have gone from questions I could not answer to answers I cannot escape." Was Jesus a maniac, or is He God in the flesh? If He is God, then everything He said about Himself is true too. We can't just pick and choose what we want.

We do not have it within ourselves to initiate a relationship with the Lord. I am radical about my faith because I have been radically touched by Christ, and I want that for everyone I know. He will honor a prayer asking for the desire to know Him, but He is the initiator of even a desire to pray that prayer. Romans 3:11 says "No one seeks for God, no not one." If I find myself seeking God, it is because He has first drawn me. The Lord woos us to Himself.

Eternity is looming on the horizon for each of us. We feel inadequate for the task and we are. It's not striving or trying on our part that saves us, but resting and trusting in the finished work of Christ on the cross for our sins. God knows we are exhausted. He simply asks us to come to Him, get real with Him, and acknowledge that we are weary and need Him to save us because we can't save ourselves. He is God; He will. "Lord I believe, help my unbelief." (Mark 9:24) It's like opening the door to a lion's cage. If we open the door and ask Him to prove Himself to us, He will. And then we can rest.

CHAPTER 7

Lessons Learned
in the School of Suffering

"Those who have suffered much are like those who know many languages;
they have learned to understand and to be understood by all."
~ Mme. Swetchine

"Though He slay me, yet will I trust Him."
~ Job 13:15

I'VE HAD A trial run at dying. Many of us avoid thinking about our own death at all costs. Instead, I allow myself to consider my own death, and it moves me to greater humility and deeper yielding to the sovereignty of God. In my favorite movie, *It's a Wonderful Life,* Clarence the angel tells George Bailey, "You have been given a great gift, George, a chance to see what the world would be like without you." These words call to mind two of the great gifts I've received: the chance to see

Joy on High Places

what my life was like without Christ and the opportunity to ponder my own mortality. Moments of destiny sometimes happen when we least expect them. Because they wrought in me a greater yieldedness to God, the events of the next few years changed the course of my life and the lives of my children and grandchildren.

Just before the time of my cancer diagnosis in 1994, I had been reading *My Utmost for His Highest*. I have to admit there were many days that I felt the truths that Oswald Chambers described were completely over my head. That was true of his discourse on November 17th. That day was to become a red letter day in my life since that was the day of my surgery. A few days after surgery, I looked back at November 17th in the devotional. When I read it, I felt completely at a loss as to what it meant, especially the Scripture quoted on that day, "Whom have I in heaven but you? And there is nothing on earth that I desire besides you." (Psalm 73:25) Well, Psalm 73 has since become one of my favorite passages. Tragedy is a great clarifier. I would come to understand in the following year exactly what that Scripture meant. When you go through deep sorrow and suffering, you realize that nothing this world has to offer satisfies the longing soul. God and God alone can do that. He meets our deepest longings in a way that nothing else was ever meant to.

I once heard it said that it's worth being sick if it means that Jesus will come to our bedside. God allows sorrow and suffering to be our companions to bring us to the high places of a relationship with Him. It is impossible to be proud when you are holding the hands of sorrow and suffering. Having such serious health issues left me in a state of brokenness, but I came to learn that when we are emptied by God, He fills our emptiness with Himself. Our brokenness comes from the hand of a perfect, loving Father. He never breaks us to leave us broken. He breaks us to fill the broken places with Himself. I was emerging weak in health but purified in spirit. I had found a source of joy that is totally independent of outside circumstances.

God used two important things to prepare me for what would be the greatest trial of my life up to that point. First, He gave me a book: *Hinds' Feet on High Places* by Hannah Hurnard. This book became a great solace to me in the weeks and months following my surgery as I struggled with fear. It seemed at times this little book contained exactly the Scripture or biblical truth I needed at the very moment I needed it. That book, along with continued immersion in Scripture, helped to keep my focus where it needed to be, on the unseen. "So we fix our eyes not on what is seen, but on what is unseen, since what is seen is temporary, but what is unseen is eternal" (2 Corinthians 4:18).

Although He doesn't always do this, I believe God asked me if I would trust Him even before He allowed such deep suffering in my life. This was the second way He prepared me for what was to come. How did He do it? Dan and I made the trek to The Cove, Billy Graham's training center, to attend a conference led by Patrick Morley, who wrote *The Man in the Mirror*. Providentially, it was the weekend before I would receive confirmation of the cancer diagnosis. As I went to the conference, I already knew that if the diagnosis came back positive, it was going to be a serious battle because of the symptoms I was already experiencing. Naturally, I was concerned and prayed a lot about it that weekend.

I remember very little about the content of Patrick Morley's talk, but what I do remember most was the breakout session we attended in a small group. The session dissected the words of Jesus when He asked, "Father, if You are willing, take this cup from Me; yet not My will but Yours be done" (Luke 22:42). "Thy will be done" is Jesus' own story of abandoning Himself to God the Father. Mary, the mother of Jesus, experienced the same surrender when she said, "Let this happen to me as you say" (Luke 1:38). Jesus' mother submitted her will to God's. How do we get from asking God to take intense suffering away from us to accepting His will for us even to the point of death? Together the class examined the book of Job. We studied the God of Job who asked, "Where were you when I laid the earth's foundation?" (Job 38:4)

As we thoroughly read and prayed through God's answer to Job, I saw that God indeed was and is completely trustworthy. I came to fully grasp the truth of Romans 14:8, "If we live, it's to honor the Lord. And if we die, it's to honor the Lord. So whether we live or die, we belong to the Lord." The speaker asked us to consider what we were asking God to let pass before us. Then he asked us if we were willing to say, "Yet not my will but Yours be done." Miraculously, I was able to do that. I told the Lord He had my permission to do whatever He wanted with me. For God to take "Little Much-Afraid Peggy Margo Wojtowicz," who had had a phobia of cancer most of her life, and bring her to a point of saying, "Yes, Lord, I accept that for me if it's what You want" was a miraculous work in my trembling heart. I came home from that conference knowing I was in God's hands no matter what lay ahead.

Today is Wednesday, October 15, 2014, almost twenty years to the day since the Lord asked me to drink the cup of suffering He allowed in my life. I drank it in communion with Him. Today I celebrate being healed and am grateful He has given me twenty years of being cancer-free. In God's providence, I am back at The Cove. As I write this, I am seated on the back porch of the Billy Graham Training Center sitting in one of the many rocking chairs facing the magnificent, rolling Blue Ridge Mountains. It is a glorious, sunny day with white puffy clouds in an azure sky and a touch of fall in the air while the mountains are ablaze with the vibrant colors of fall. My friend, Mary, is volunteering her time here, and I am privileged to be here as her guest. When Mary invited me to come with her, I recognized this as a gift that the Lord has allowed me come back to this mountain to finish this portion of my memoir.

Although I was a strong believer before going through cancer, clearly that was a turning point in my life of living the exchanged life in Christ, my life for His. I learned that year that we may experience situations where our body and soul are broken, but our spirit is soaring. That would explain a verse like 2 Corinthians 6:10, in which Paul describes extreme physical hardship and suffering of the soul and yet proclaims how he was "sorrowful, yet always rejoicing." J.I. Packer puts it this way: "Pain and suffering are God's chisel for sculpting our lives. Weakness deepens our dependence on Christ for strength each day. The weaker we feel, the harder we lean; the harder we lean, the stronger we grow spiritually even while our bodies waste away." (*Knowing God*)

An endless source of comfort came from the body of Christ, friends who ministered to me as the hands of God. I live far from my nearest family members. While they offered to come and care for me, my friends were the ones who stood in the gap and taught me much about what it means to show love and "bear one another's burdens." The outpouring of love was overwhelming.

I began receiving chemotherapy in mid-December, and by Christmas Eve my hair was falling out in clumps and I was experiencing severe nausea and vomiting. I eventually lost all my hair, and I started to wear a baseball cap until the wig I had ordered arrived. Pastor Steve's wife, Pat, asked if she could come by for a visit. When she arrived, she explained that she and Steve knew that I had a long road ahead of me, and they wanted to be sure that I never felt forgotten. To remind me that I was in their thoughts and prayers, she would be visiting me weekly. Pat explained that she would deliver a different hat to me each week. These hats or baseball caps weren't necessarily to be worn but rather were a sweet reminder of their support of me. Each hat was accompanied by a brief note from them. The very first hat was a bee keeper's hat. The note read, "We will *bee keeping* our eyes on you as you keep your eyes on Him." How absolutely delightful and touching. There were so many hats that followed but one of my other favorites was a Braves baseball cap with a note that simply read, "Be Brave!"

My incredible best friend, Sheilah, supported me in more ways than I can name, but one act of love humbled me and spoke volumes to me about what it meant to be a true, sacrificial friend. Although she was the mother of two young children, each and every week Sheilah drove 2½ hours each way to spend the day with me, often bearing a gift for me, only to turn around and drive home that same day. Kristi and Liz offered to pray for me any time I felt the need for special support.

Knowing how drained and weary I might be, Kristi told me to just give her a brief call (pre-text messaging) and simply say, "Today is a 10" meaning a very bad day and I really needed help. Without requiring more information than that, they would immediately begin to pray.

Another outpouring of love started the week preceding Christmas. Each evening of that week we had gifts anonymously left on our front porch. Each gift was accompanied by a short note of inspiration or verse of Scripture. These thoughtful gifts ministered to our entire family, and the kids loved it. We were surprised one evening with a bundle of wood for our fireplace and packets of instant hot chocolate. Another evening, to our delight, we found two loaves of freshly baked homemade bread. "See, I have written your name on the palms of my hands" (Isaiah 49:16) was one of the many beautiful verses I received that week. Another gift was a large, adorable teddy bear. Mr. Teddy Bear held a note entitled *A Tandem Ride with God*, which describes us taking the back seat in life as Jesus takes the lead and simply asks us to keep pedaling.

Fran was a friend of another dear friend and mentor, Reggie, and it was humbling to know that they prayed together on my behalf. The following note came from her, a lady I never met but one who prayed much for me.

"*As members of His body we suffer with you and truly want His very best for you and yours. What that 'best' is I don't know – and perhaps at this time you, too, are groping for that answer. Lean hard on Romans 8:28 and 29. It often seems all too easy for folks to quote that 28th verse to us when we're desperately crying out in the dark, doesn't it – but it should never be quoted without the following verse to which it is connected by 'For' or 'because.' How do I know that however desperate my case may seem to be He is definitely going to bring this very thing to contribute to His great purpose for me? 'Because' when He chose me for the mind boggling future for which I was created – that, as Philips translates it, 'I may bear the family likeness of His Son' – predestined to be like Jesus Christ in order that we may reflect His beauty forever and ever and delight the heart of God the Father as He sees him multiplied over and over.*

Now, tell me, with a purpose like that in His mind could He let anything – anything – come to us that was not working toward that plan and purpose? He is making you like His Firstborn.

No, my dear, I haven't any idea how it can be within the perfect plan for a loving and needed wife and mother to have to cope with such a dreaded disease and be very sure I'm asking Him to bring about healing through whatever means He chooses to use. In the meantime, however, I am praying that "the trial of your faith," and that's surely what this is for you all, may strengthen you in your trust of Him. After all, He gave Heaven's best for you and that forbids us to think that He'll ever let you slip out of His hands and His plans, doesn't it?"

The year 1994 turned out to be the most sorrowful and the most blessed year of my life up to that point. Hudson Taylor, founder of the China Inland Mission, wrote these words soon after the death of his beloved wife, Maria, and infant son. I repeat his words, "It has been the most sorrowful and the most blessed year of my life. We have put to the proof the faithfulness of God – His power to support in trouble and affliction...and should deeper sorrows come it is hoped they will be met in a strengthened confidence in our God." I also agree with the words of A. W. Tozer when he said, "I have tasted of Your goodness, and it has both satisfied me and made me thirst for more."

Perhaps the most priceless lesson I learned that year was that God, and God alone, was what my heart most desired. John Piper says, "When the promise IS the Promised, you are satisfied in the Promised as well as believing the trustworthiness of the Promiser. The Promiser is the Promised." God promised to take me through this trial and He did. He asked me to give myself and in return He gave me Himself. This must have been what the poet D. M. McIntyre had in mind when he wrote the following:

> Lord, here I hold within my trembling hand,
> This will of mine--a thing which seems small;
> And only Thou, O Christ, can understand
> How, when I yield You this, I yield my all.
> It has been wet with tears, and stained with sighs,

Clenched in my grasp till beauty it has none;
Now, from Your footstool where it prostrate lies
The prayer ascends, Let Thy will be done.

On trusting God through unexplained trying circumstances, Amy Carmichael wrote the following: "I have been thinking of how many unexplained things there are in life. Our Lord Jesus Who could have explained everything, explained nothing. He said there would be tribulation, but He never said why. Sometimes He spoke of suffering being to the glory of God, but He never said how. All through the Scriptures it is the same. I cannot recall a single explanation of trial. We are trusted with the unexplained! May the Lord strengthen us all in every little call on faith as well as in every great call, so to live in patience and steadfastness, that the trial of our faith...may be found unto praise and honor and glory at the appearing of our Lord Jesus Christ, Whom having not seen we love." – Amy Carmichael

I had plenty of time to lie physically still while receiving six weeks of daily radiation treatments. The resulting burns to my skin reminded me of a favorite verse, Isaiah 43:2-4, which refers to going through the fire. I memorized this verse and meditated on it while lying on the treatment table. "Fear not, for I have redeemed you; I have called you by name, you are mine. When you pass through the waters, I will be with you; and through the rivers, they shall not overwhelm you; when you walk through fire you shall not be burned, and the flame shall not consume you. For I am the LORD your God, the Holy One of Israel, your

Savior...you are precious in my eyes, and honored, and I love you."

Hannah Whitall Smith wrote in *The God of All Comfort*: "The last and greatest lesson that the soul has to learn is the fact that God, and God alone, is enough for all its needs. This is the lesson that all His dealings with us are meant to teach; and this is the crowning discovery of our whole Christian life. God is enough! No soul can be really at rest until it has given up all dependence on everything else and has been forced to depend on the Lord alone. As long as our expectation is from other things, nothing but disappointment awaits us. Feelings may change and will change with our changing circumstances; doctrines and dogmas may be upset; Christian work may come to naught; prayers may seem to lose their fervency; promises may seem to fail; everything that we have believed in or depended upon may seem to be swept away, and only God is left, just God...simply and only God. The soul is made for this and can never find rest short of it. All God's dealings with us, therefore, are shaped to this end; and He is often obliged to deprive us of all joy in everything else in order that He may force us to find our joy only and altogether in Himself."

CHAPTER 8

Slow Down or You Might Fall and Break Your Neck

GOD PERMITS WHAT He hates in order to accomplish that which He loves. Look at what God permitted at the cross: treason, torture, murder. We might ask how any of that can be the Father's will. Acts 4:27-28 addresses this dilemma:

> "for truly in this city there were gathered together against your holy servant, Jesus, whom you anointed, both Herod and Pontius Pilate, along with the Gentiles and the peoples of Israel, to do whatever your hand and your plan had predestined to take place."

What could the Father prize more than His own son? Our salvation. Suffering is the textbook that will teach you who you really are.

Through our trials we are like lemons: God squeezes us, and out comes the cranky crabbiness, the sour disposition, the peevish attitude. When we discover what is really inside us we say "I don't want to be that person" and "I can't do this, Jesus, but you can."

Another season of physical pain for me began on January 2, 2017. I started the new year out with a bang, quite literally. I was walking to my car in the driveway. I tripped over a sprinkler head and fell, hitting my head on a parked car and sustaining two fractured vertebrae in my neck (C2 and C3) as well as a bruised vertebral artery. While the prognosis was that I would make a complete recovery after several months wearing a neck brace and taking blood thinners, it was one of the most physically painful and trying experiences of my life. It was shocking to me and everyone around me how quickly life could take a turn. One minute I was Party Peggy, getting ready to celebrate being with my family, and the next thing I knew I had sustained the worst injury I'd ever had, simply by walking to my car. I thought about God's hand of protection on me even then, as I learned that many people either become paralyzed or simply do not recover from an injury of this type. I thought about how I had safely participated in many much riskier events: horseback riding, snow skiing, waterskiing, hiking along cliffs, and taking multiple trips to the Central African Republic, the country currently listed as the most dangerous country in the world for outside travelers.

A ten-day hospital stay – which included lying flat on a bed for three days and nights until an arteriogram could confirm there was no cerebral bleeding – left me feeling deeply isolated. A sprained left arm and a right arm full of IV's made it impossible to use my hands to feed myself or use my phone to communicate. I had to rely completely on others. Due to the neck brace, I couldn't even turn my head to look at the doctors and nurses treating me unless they positioned themselves directly over my bed. I literally had nowhere to look except up.

And God did not disappoint. My sweet times of listening to Him and receiving peace against all odds are times I would never trade. When you feel desperate and helpless, leave the door open for God to amaze you with His provision. He will. And when He does, it will startle you and fortify you in a way that no one else can. It will be one of myriad experiences that will strengthen your faith until your joy in Him is unquenchable and your faith in Him unshakable.

The gift of a broken neck – is that what I would have chosen for myself? Hardly, but then again I didn't choose it. It was a cup the Father in His sovereign omniscience chose for me. Jesus, God's own Son, declared in the Garden of Gethsemane that His suffering was God's idea. "So Jesus said to Peter, 'Put your sword into its sheath; shall I not drink the cup that the Father has given Me?'" Every single one of us drinks a cup that we didn't choose for ourselves. We can either drink it alone and be miserable or drink it in communion with Him and be sustained.

Part of the benefit of experiencing this sort of thing is the privilege of sharing my perspective from my hospital bed. There are times when the Word of God reads like honey and coats our lives like a sweet balm.

One of the benefits of reading and studying God's Word is that it builds a reservoir of truth for God to bring to your mind when you need it. Without a word from anyone else, God brought to mind two verses that helped to sustain me throughout, but especially in the hours before pain medicine. These were times when I was being jostled around, transferred in two different ambulances to two different hospitals, and moved from table to table for scans. He called to my mind Song of Solomon 2:6: "His left arm is under my head, and His right arm embraces me." Did that mean nothing bad was going to happen to me? No, it meant that my anxiety about health workers handling me correctly and the pain I experienced was dissipated by that overriding truth. It was His hands I was relaxing in, not theirs. When you cannot find solace in the arms of someone else, His arms will never fail you. At the moment my head hit the car, God's left arm was under my head and His right arm embraced me. He never dropped me. During those first trying hours He reminded me also of the truth of His Word in Psalm 3:4: "But you, O LORD, are a shield about me, my glory, and the lifter of my head."

Joni Eareckson Tada has long been a favorite author and speaker of mine. At the tender age of 17, a diving accident left Joni a quadriplegic in a wheelchair. After two years of rehabilitation, Joni emerged with new skills and a fresh determination to help others in similar situations. She has become an international advocate for people with disabilities. Although I continually thanked God that I was not left paralyzed by this accident, this was still the closest in my life I had ever come to truly empathizing with Joni, and I longed to hear from her. When I needed it most during the wee hours of the morning of the fourth day in the hospital, I was finally able to fumble with my phone and pull up one of her podcasts, which gave me great encouragement.

> "In Jeremiah 29 when God says He will not harm us, it doesn't mean our body. It doesn't mean our circumstances. He's not going to do anything to harm our soul. Yes, our body may get harmed, but it will somehow serve to enrich our soul. Suffering is like little splashovers of hell waking us up out of our spiritual slumber. So are splashovers of heaven those easy, breezy bright times where everything is going your way? No. Splashovers of heaven are finding Jesus in your splashover of hell. And to find Jesus in your hell is ecstasy beyond compare and I wouldn't trade it for any amount of walking [health] in this world." (*Joni Eareckson Tada Shares Her Story*)

It's been my habit to say that there is a sweetness accompanying the bitterness of suffering, so these become seasons we look back on as bittersweet. It's impossible to overstate how much sweetness my adult kids brought me during this season of trial. They simply shone! I am living the promise of the Lord when He declared, "Children are a gift from the Lord; they are a reward from Him." (Psalm 127:3-5, NLT) According to numerous passages in the book of Proverbs, having adult children is intended to be a time of relishing the product of all the years of our labor. Raising children to a true biblical definition of adulthood results in children who are not only physically and financially independent of us, but are independently dependent on Jesus Christ. The beautiful demonstration of that type of maturity in my adult children is what I had the privilege of witnessing. Ashley and Aaron not only comforted and encouraged me, they downright inspired me.

Aaron is the kind of guy who never appears flustered. He has a steady, easygoing demeanor which is endearing and calming. Like a duck gliding along a tranquil pond who is actually paddling like a madman under the surface, Aaron has a knack for keeping his head when others lose theirs. A memory which I am sure will stay with me forever is of Aaron placing his hand on my shoulder and praying for me before the ambulance took me away. Aaron's level-headed thinking and tongue-in-cheek humor brightened my hospital stay and made me proud as a mom. When his four-year-old daughter, Riley, whispered something in his ear on one of their hospital visits, Aaron gave her permission to do what she had asked. At that, she took hold of my hand and her daddy's hand and prayed for me. It doesn't get much better than watching your kids and grandkids gathering around you and praying for you in your time of need.

Ashley is a worker bee and servant at heart, so restraining her from jumping on a plane and coming to my aid was a major task. Although I finally won the battle for her to stay home, in the beginning Ashley insisted on traveling from coast to coast to be by my side in spite of the fact that she had three small children: two in diapers and one who was nursing and couldn't bear to be away from Mama. From 2,000 miles away I felt Ashley's heart for me and knew it was very difficult for her not to be with us in person and care for me. I truly meant it when I told Ashley that distance was meaningless as she prayed for me and acted as my lighthouse from afar.

Although I had an army of helpers to cheer me and help with a million physical tasks, what I craved most was the spiritual nourishment and inspiration I got from my kids. A peek out of Ashley's window at her home near Tacoma, Washington displays picturesque Mount Rainier, majestic and uplifting. Like most mountain peaks, Mt. Rainier is obscured by cloud coverage much of the time. Faith is required to believe God's promises even when we don't see them just as we refuse to doubt that the mountain is there, huge and strong, even when totally obscured from view. Throughout those difficult days in the hospital, Ashley sent me photos of the mountain as it made its grand but rare appearances from its cloud-obscured hiding place. She kept me fed with special songs and inspiring messages from some of my favorite speakers. It made this mother's heart proud to hear repeated praises from family and friends who were so touched and impressed by my kids as they stayed in touch with extended family and friends and gave frequent updates to all involved.

There were too many sweet points along the way to enumerate them, but I do remember a few highlights: my son laying his hand on my shoulder and praying for me before the ambulance took me away, my four-year-old granddaughter, Riley, holding my hand and praying for me at the hospital, and a team of steadfast family and friends who encouraged my faith and rallied around me in amazing demonstrations of love.

One night, after I'd quietly endured being poked and prodded every few hours by nurses' aides and lab technicians, the tech came to take blood work at 5:00 a.m. Knowing they were also going to take it again at 7:30, my nurse, Rena, came running into my room and told the tech there was no reason to stick me twice. She asked the 5:00 a.m. technician to come back at 7:30, which she did. Having someone fight for me and show me that simple kindness made me cry. When Rena told me to go back to sleep and turned out the light, I lay there in the dark crying at the common humanity she was displaying toward me. When I thanked her for being there and protecting me like that, she said, "Well, that's why I'm here, sweetie: to take the best care of you."

The look on my face and the tears in my eyes reflected a look I've witnessed many times when ministering to others. It was a common expression in Africa, in women and children overwhelmed with gratitude at the smallest kindnesses done for them. I've been brought to mutual tears with my widowed African sisters when I washed their feet and lovingly put new sandals on them, or held a child who is not used to such displays of tenderness or affection. The human spirit can be so fragile at times that a gentle word or kindness can be overwhelming. Be kind even when others aren't. Be gentle. Depletion of our inner strength happens daily and accelerates during times of stress and trial.

I have learned in life that a pool of self-pity is a miserable place to be, but, more importantly, it is not from God. The way to fight self-pity is to acknowledge our loss, offering it up to Him, and then to get busy about the task of praising Him for the blessings that we do have. A song that helps me do this while building courage in me is called "You Make Me Brave" by Amanda Cook. I love the lyrics:

I have heard You calling my name
I have heard the song of love that You sing
So I will let You draw me out beyond the shore
Into Your grace
Your grace

You make me brave
You make me brave
You call me out beyond the shore into the waves
You make me brave
You make me brave
No fear can hinder now the love that made a way

As Your love, in wave after wave
Crashes over me, crashes over me
For You are for us
You are not against us
Champion of Heaven
You made a way for all to enter in

Although my dad had passed away many years earlier, his example brought me courage during this time of testing. I grew up hearing stories from my dad about how he had broken his neck in World War II, years before he married my mom. Dad was in the Army, stationed in Rome, when he and his peers were given a few days of leave or R&R. He always made a point of pointing out that he was being a good boy and passed up the drinking and womanizing his fellow soldiers planned for their time on leave. Instead, dad decided to go swimming in the Tiber River. Seeing local Italian women washing clothes at the edge of the river, dad walked to the end of a very long dock. Assuming the muddy water was deep, he dove head first into what turned out to be just two feet of water. He lost consciousness and would have drowned if not for the local women who alerted several Military Police who, as he put it, "fished him out."

He sustained three displaced, fractured cervical vertebrae. Considering he was facing such serious injuries in 1940's Italy, it's truly amazing he survived with no lasting ill effects. But that's not to say that he didn't have a long road to recovery. He was originally placed in a body cast, which he found horribly uncomfortable. Later, he graduated to a neck brace. In September 1944, Dad was shipped stateside on a hospital ship and ended up at Fort Story in Virginia Beach, Virginia. He was discharged from the Army in April 1946 from Rhoads Army Hospital in Utica, New York.

When my brother heard that I had endured a ten day hospital stay, his letter brought a touch of humor: "Glad you are making headway.

After all, it took Dad from September 1944 to April 1946 to fully rehab. Medicine has made strides, thank God!" Those photos of my Dad in his cast and neck brace served as a source of courage and strength when I think of the greater trauma he endured and how he lived to regale us with his tale.

I learned that during times of trial, it is imperative that we flee temptation. We will be tempted to fill up our broken places with everything but God. We may seek deliverance through a divorce, an affair, wine, gluttony, shopping, an abortion, or any number of other means, but whatever the specific situation, in every case Satan will tempt us to escape the pain that comes with walking by faith in Christ through our trials. He tempted Jesus the same way, with bread in the desert (Matthew 4:3). But Christ leads by example and calls us to cling to God's word and follow Him (Matthew 4:4, 7, 10). These temptations will come flooding in, trying to fill the broken places. If we are not careful, we can find it easier to look to those things to temporarily fill us up. But that's just the problem. Their anesthesia is temporary at best, addictive and destructive at worst. Those choices can lead us to feel more desperate than ever.

Refreshment and times of ease definitely have their place. I certainly am not saying it's wrong to enjoy the good gifts given to us from above. "There is nothing better for a person than that he should eat and drink and find enjoyment in his toil. This also, I saw, is from the hand of God" (Ecclesiastes 2:24). But their joy is fleeting; His is eternal. It takes wisdom to know the difference. God's Word says in Colossians 3:2, "Set your minds on things that are above, not on things that are on earth." When God is calling you to look to Him, don't drown Him out with other things.

I also found that one of the most trying aspects of times of trial is how much we have to rely on one another. We all want to be independent, and leaning on other people is tough for most of us. Just like many people, I enjoy ministering to others in their time of need. It truly is often better to give than to receive. But the Lord has taught me that He often wants to humble us by making us reliant on others.

A young lady who knows me well and is like a daughter to me, Laura, reminded me of this early on. When she came to visit me and help me on one of my first days home from the hospital, I greeted her with a teary-eyed hug. "Oh, so you can dish it out but you can't take it, huh?" she kidded. I knew instantly what she meant. We all want to be on the serving end of a relationship as opposed to being served. This was a time that God was calling me to be a patient patient – pun intended – and to graciously allow myself to be served.

CHAPTER 9

Living as a New Creation

"And I will give you a new heart, and a new spirit I will put within you. And I will remove the heart of stone from your flesh and give you a heart of flesh. And I will put My Spirit within you, and cause you to walk in my statutes and be careful to obey My rules."
- Ezekiel 36:26-27

"He must increase, but I must decrease."
- John 3:30

THE BOOK OF John tells the story of Jesus raising Lazarus from the dead. Although Lazarus had been dead for three days, at Christ's command he came out of the grave. But he was still in bondage. "The dead man came out, his hands and feet wrapped with strips of linen, and a cloth around his face. Jesus said to them, 'Take off the grave clothes and let him go'." (John 11:44)

My friend and mentor, Beth, makes the observation that although

Lazarus had new life, he could not take off his own grave clothes. He needed someone to do that for him. It seems to me that we are in much the same predicament as Lazarus. Although we may have new life in Christ, there is still a stench about us as we are bound by our grave clothes. Although we are a new creation in Christ, we may be bound with the habits and addictions of the old man. "Therefore, if anyone is in Christ, he is a new creation. The old has passed away; behold, the new has come" (2 Corinthians 5:17). Just as surely as Jesus calling the name of Lazarus, I have heard Him call my name. I have let Him call me out beyond the shore into His grace. He makes me brave.

I was no different from Lazarus. But "the Lord knows how to deliver the godly out of temptations." (2 Peter 2:9) Although I now had a new nature in Christ and had His life living in me, the old man was still bound by habits unbecoming my new nature, habits like profanity, excessive drinking, smoking, overeating, and uncontrolled anger. I could not remove these grave clothes myself. That was God's job. But I had to cooperate with Him.

I also have to resist any unwillingness to come to Him in confession of my sin. If we see God as accusatory, harsh, and condemning, then our view of God is the Bible's view of Satan. Satan, not God, is all of those things. God is love. If we see God as unwilling to forgive sin, then Satan has duped us.

According to Ann Voskamp, author of *One Thousand Gifts*, "Our endless desires are fulfilled in an endless God." She was correct when she said that we have endless desires. All too often those desires come from our flesh, which wants to be satisfied, and the consequences can be dire. We become slaves to ourselves. We do the thing we do not want to do. How do I do what I ought to do rather than what I want? According to Erasmus, "A nail is driven out by another nail. Habit is overcome by habit." I have found this to be true. If I want to give up a bad habit, it seems it is best replaced by something good.

One day I was given a visible demonstration of this principle. In 1995, the same year I underwent chemotherapy and radiation, I was facilitating a group called Friendship Bible Coffee on Philippians at my next door neighbor's house. We were discussing 2 Corinthians 4:14: "Therefore we do not lose heart. Though outwardly we are wasting away, yet inwardly we are being renewed day by day." The study explained that though the young pin oak tree's leaves turn brown and die in the fall, it retains the dead leaves through the winter. It's only the fresh growth of new leaves in the spring that gently pushes the old, dead leaves off to make room for the new ones. The point was made that trying to put off the old man is virtually impossible unless one is building up the new, inner man. As we shift our focus off the unwanted, ungodly habits and fix our eyes on getting to know the Lord, the inner man strengthens, grows and pushes off the old, dead man. As we were studying this principle, we looked out the window to see that, in a remarkable coincidence, there stood a young pin oak tree, brown leaves and all, in her back yard as our object lesson.

God is a God of breakthroughs, and I am a trophy of His abundant grace. Being released from the slavery of these "besetting sins" has been a process. I'm forever grateful that early in my walk with the Lord, our friend, Mike, encouraged us to memorize Scripture. He showed me Psalm 119 which says, "How can a young man [or woman] stay pure? By reading Your Word and following its rules. I have thought much about Your Words and stored them in my heart so that they would hold me back from sin." (119:9-11). I began to memorize Scripture, since I also learned that "The Word of God is alive and powerful. It is sharper than the sharpest two-edged sword, cutting between soul and spirit, between joint and marrow. It exposes our innermost thoughts and desires." (Hebrews 4:12)

Job says he desired God's Word "more than my necessary food." I began to crave God's Word as I saw its power to change me. In my old life, I built idols and practices that were harmful to me. Two of the Scriptures that meant so much to me when I was struggling to give up cigarettes were 2 Kings 18: "And [she] did what was right in the sight of the Lord...[She] trusted in the Lord God of Israel...[She] broke the sacred pillars" and "Behold, I am the Lord, the God of all flesh. Is there anything too hard for me?" (Jeremiah 32:27)

Sin promises joy but produces sorrow. We need to love God so much that we side with Him against ourselves. God is for us more than we are for ourselves. One of the times the Lord drove this home with me occurred when I picked Ashley up from first grade one day. She had been playing on the school playground, and when she slid off the old, wooden see-saw, four large splinters pierced her thumb and lodged themselves under her fingernail. It soon became clear a doctor would have to remove them. She was not in pain and was her happy-go-lucky little self, animated and brightly chatting about her fun day at school, but as I drove her to the doctor's office, my stomach was in a knot as I thought about how painful it was going to be to get those splinters out and how large the needle would be to anesthetize the area. Any parent who has been through a similar situation knows exactly what I mean. Even though I knew it was necessary, her big, green tear-filled eyes pleading with me to make the doctor stop as he painstakingly dug out those splinters just about made my heart break.

We are that little child refusing to let our Father pull out a splinter. The child, who is for himself, doesn't want to hurt. The father is even more for the child than the child himself. He does not want the child to hurt, or get an infection. He loves his child enough to cause the necessary pain that will bring needed healing. The child needs to love and trust his father "against" his trust of himself.

Psalm 118:27 brought this home to me. "The LORD is God, and He has made his light to shine upon us. Bind the festal sacrifice with cords, up to the horns of the altar!" The sacrifice we present is ourselves, a living sacrifice of our spirit, body, and soul. "Tie me down if you must, Lord," I have said to Him, "but don't let me do anything that will go against your will." This ache of my heart is reflected in my journal note of December 5, 1994. It reads, "I feel a wrenching of my mind, will, and emotions; a handing over to Him. Letting go, surrendering so much, but in exchange for even more. Pride, self-will, my own capabilities are all things I'm being asked to surrender. The picture of a splinter being removed from my body. The pain of having it removed and yet my desire is to have it removed. Tie me down if you must, but remove all that is not pleasing to You from me."

When he was just a young man, the son of my longtime friend and prayer partner, Beth, wrote a stirring poem depicting this battle for supremacy in our lives.

Christ is Winning and He's Won!
by David Watson

When I feel the devil's breath on the collar of my shirt,
When I hear his filthy whisp'ring with all its grime and dirt,
When he plants within my mind and soul a deep rooted fear,
I can rest assured my Savior, Jesus, will not desert, He is near.
When the devil fights for you and the devil fights for me,
Sometimes it seems as though he is winning and might have the victory.
When the battlefield is raging and it's Satan against God's Son,
Fear not, weary Christian, Christ is winning and He's won!

The Pharisees, during the time of Christ, said "Change and then follow us." Actually, many modern-day Pharisees say the same. But being a Christian is not about following rules. It is a relationship. Jesus says, "Follow me and you will change." Being a sinner does not disqualify me from following Jesus. It is a prerequisite. Jesus called only sinners to repentance. It is God's kindness demonstrated through Christ that leads us to repentance or change. Is change hard? You better believe it! As a matter of fact, I would say true change is almost impossible apart from the power of God to change us. One of the biggest temptations for a believer is to do what is easy rather than what is right. According to Pastor Steve, "Grace is God giving us the desire, power, and ability to do what He has called us to do."

In 2 Peter 2:9 it says, "The Lord knows how to deliver the godly out of temptations." The Lord proved this to me when I had final victory over my smoking addiction. After many failed attempts, I finally became desperate enough in 1989 to come clean with this addiction. Up until that point, many of my Christian friends didn't even know that I smoked. I didn't intend to keep them in the dark about that, but I didn't smoke in public and the longer they knew me the harder it was to blurt out, "By the way, I'm a smoker and I need help." Sin grows in the dark. Satan's ploy is to keep us so ashamed of our sin that we hide it and become isolated from the very help we need: the prayers and account-ability of others. I needed help removing those grave clothes!

I have poignant memories of the day I finally humbled myself and asked for help. I was sick and tired of being sick and tired. I was in a ladies' Bible study, and when it came time for prayer requests, I admitted that I had been smoking for years and wanted the prayers of the group to help me be free at last. It was definitely an act of humbling myself before others because, as I expected, they were shocked. Their response, however, was wonderful. They were so supportive and earnestly prayed for me. The transparency I displayed by coming clean also gave several others boldness to ask for prayer for some of their secret struggles. People connect with vulnerability.

I set a quit date and stuck to it. I had plenty of people praying for me. I knew the first week would be the most trying, so I planned a multitude of fun activities to keep me busy. Wednesday of that week was the only day I had nothing scheduled, and it made me a little uneasy to leave that day free. But God encouraged me so much when my best friend, Sheilah, called to say she was going to be in Aiken that day and could I possibly spend the day with her? Could I!

Another confirmation of God's orchestration was when I went to work at the end of the week. Ironically, the doctor I worked for was also a smoker. His office was the one place I knew I would be tempted, since he often smoked at my desk at the end of the day and left cigarettes lying around the office. I bolstered myself and walked in the back door to his private office. The normally smoke-filled room was oddly devoid of smoke. I didn't see any ash trays or cigarettes lying around either. As I stood there trying to take it all in, he walked into the room. I asked him about the lack of smoke and cigarettes.

He said, "Oh, didn't I tell you? I quit smoking this week while we were on vacation. I've had it planned a long time. I thought I told you I was going to quit."

I couldn't help myself as I almost yelled, "Praise God!"

He was startled as I'm sure he thought, "I didn't know you cared so much."

I told him that God had done the same for me! He and I had a good laugh about the fact that we had both quit in the same week, unbeknownst to one another.

CHAPTER 10

The Road to Transformation

"LORD, I have heard of your fame; I stand in awe of your deeds."
~ *Habakkuk 3:2*

"Fools do not learn from their mistakes and experiences. Smart people learn
from their mistakes and experiences. The wise learn from the mistakes and
experiences of others."
~ *Anonymous*

ACCORDING TO JOHN Piper, when you come to Christ, "the temple of
your soul is filled with idols and the smashing of those idols by the new
Lord of the temple will be a lifelong experience of happy pain." The next
step after salvation is our never-ending sanctification of becoming more
like Christ. Having failed to keep me from the gospel, Satan tries to keep
the gospel from coming through me. But God desires me to grow in
Christlikeness. This change is not an act of the will, but rather a work
of the Holy Spirit. Paul writes in Galatians 3:1-3, "O foolish Galatians!

Who has bewitched you? It was before your eyes that Jesus Christ was publicly portrayed as crucified. Let me ask you only this: Did you receive the Spirit by works of the law or by hearing with faith? Are you so foolish? Having begun by the Spirit, are you now being perfected by the flesh?"

This process of becoming more Christ-like is one that continues until we die. Although it is never a one-time thing, there are those times when God changes us radically. St. Augustine experienced this when he said, "How sweet all at once it was for me to be rid of those fruitless joys which I had once feared to lose! You drove them from me, You Who are the True, the Sovereign Joy. You drove them from me and took their place, You Who are sweeter than all pleasure." Martin Luther says, "We are not yet what we shall be."

When I moved to the South I met a plant I have come to dislike: kudzu. Kudzu is a weed that was originally planted to help halt erosion. That decision has had devastating environmental consequences. Kudzu has become known as "the vine that ate the South." I often feel like I'm dealing with kudzu in my life as I try to escape my flesh and its never-ending propensity to be in bondage to the things of this world. "The Lord brought [us] out of Egypt, from the house of bondage" (Deuteronomy 6:12), and He continues to deliver us from the life-sucking tendrils of the kudzu of this world.

True change does not happen without repentance. This lesson was made clear to me when Dan taught a Sunday School class on a book called, *Don't Just Stand There, Pray Something* by Ronald Dunn. The author told of a day he was praying like a wimp. His dialogue with God went something like this, "Lord I know I have no right to ask you for anything tonight." He proceeded to apologize for being too busy that day to do anything "spiritual." It seemed as if the Lord asked him, "Would you feel more confident praying if you had read your Bible for three hours and led ten people to Christ today?" He thought for a minute and exclaimed, "Yes, I would." It was then that he realized that the throne room of the Holy of Holies was sprinkled with the blood of Christ, not with the sweat of his own good works. We have to remember that true repentance and deliverance don't come from our own heroic efforts but from the blood of Christ. We cannot buy into the lie that we are unworthy to cry out to God. Transformation is based not on our worth but on the worth of Christ.

In trying to make ourselves good enough for God, we miss the real power of the gospel. Instead of just externally "cleaning up our act," we need to stop using excuses and call our sins what they truly are. According to Paulo Coelho, "A mistake repeated more than once is a decision." The blood of Christ does not cleanse excuses but it always cleanses sin.

On this road to true change and transformation, I've found comfort in the words of an old Puritan saying: "Delighting in Him may be the work of our lives. This joy will arm us against the assaults of our spiritual enemies and put our mouths out of taste for those pleasures with which the tempter baits his hooks."

Romans 12:1-2 reminds me that although I may be a strong person by constitution, ultimately the work of change is His not mine. "I beseech you therefore, brethren, by the mercies of God, that you present your bodies a living sacrifice, holy, acceptable to God, which is your reasonable service. And do not be conformed to this world, but be transformed by the renewing of your mind, that you may prove what *is* that good and acceptable and perfect will of God."

Who is winning the battle for the will? My nature is to demand my right to myself. The moment I am willing to let God change my nature, His recreating forces will begin to work. I can't fill with joy until I learn how to trust. "Now, may the God of hope fill you with all joy and peace in believing, that you may abound in hope by the power of the Holy Spirit" (Romans 15:13).

Charles Stanley, the pastor of First Baptist Church Atlanta, says, "God has no favorites, but He does have intimates. That is important. He is partial to no one, but He does seek for men and women whose hearts are wholly devoted to Him, who love Him sweetly, dearly, and passionately." The prayer and desire of my heart, O Lord, is to be one of those with whom You are intimate. We know that it's often through trials that God brings about this transformation. "Yes, we had the sentence of death in ourselves [brought to the brink of death.] Why? That we should not trust in ourselves but in God who raises the dead." (2 Corinthians 1:9)

The only real way to lasting change is through an awareness of our "missing the mark" followed by repentance and being empowered by the Holy Spirit to change course and head in a different direction. Often

Satan makes us feel so guilty and defeated that it seems easier to stay in our sinful ways than to change. We might also feel like God is so full of wrath that He can't, or won't, forgive us. Nothing could be further from the truth.

I remember a story told by speaker Ken Davis. He tells about his four-year-old granddaughter getting lost in the woods for 3½ hours and how terrified he and his family were as they searched for her. When he finally found her, do you think he started yelling at her and chastising her? No, he ran up to her, knelt down, and hugged her while tearfully repeating, "I love you, I love you, I love you!" Ken reminds us that this is the way God feels about each one of His lost sheep. When His lost sheep are found, He doesn't respond with anger or chastisement, but with overwhelming love.

Obedience is also necessary on the path to lasting change. The more we know of God and obey His commands, the more of Himself He will reveal to us. "Whoever has my commands and keeps them is the one who loves me. The one who loves me will be loved by my Father, and I too will love them and show myself to them." (John 14:21) The movie *Chariots of Fire* is based on the life of Eric Liddell, the Scottish Olympic athlete and missionary. His story is one of obedience to God in extremely difficult circumstances. Liddell writes, "One word stands out from all others as the key to knowing God, to having His peace and assurance in your heart; it is obedience. Take obedience with you into your time of prayer and meditation, for you will know as much of God, and only as much of God, as you are willing to put into practice." It isn't what you know that counts; it's what you *do* with what you know. Better a little bit of know and a lot of do, than a little do and a lot of know.

CHAPTER 11

Becoming a Woman of Moderation

"Discouragement comes when you forget what God did yesterday because you're looking at your circumstances today."
~ Pastor Tony Evans

"From whence comes my help? My help comes from the Lord."
~ Psalm 121:1

I THINK GOD takes gluttony seriously when He says in Proverbs, "put a knife to your throat if you are given to gluttony." (23:2) Even as I write this, exercising and maintaining a healthy weight is an area of my life that is still a work in progress. I've been active all my life, and I've exercised regularly, either walking or going to the gym, and this seemed to maintain my weight reasonably well until my mid-30s. After I quit smoking, I joined the gym using the same amount of money I spent on cigarettes per month to pay for the membership. Unfortunately, I still managed to gain 14 lbs. I remember my pastor's wife saying that when you overcome one bad habit, it seems there are five more that pop up right behind it. Weight gain was hiding behind smoking cessation.

To add insult to injury, I managed to gain another 16 lbs. over the next few years, leaving me with a total weight gain of 30 lbs. 1 Corinthians 6:19-20 became convicting verses: "Or do you not know that your body is a temple of the Holy Spirit within you, whom you have from God? You are not your own, for you were bought with a price. So glorify God in your body." I want to have more of an appetite for the Lord than for the things He created.

In 2010 I facilitated a Bible study by Dee Brestin called *Women of Moderation.* God is the Creator of my body, and surely He knows what will make it the healthiest, so it only makes sense to look to Him for answers to weight struggles. The thing I lacked the most was motivation. To be honest, we all know *how* to lose weight, but it's having the consistent *desire* to do it that is missing in most of our lives. I was no different. Philippians 2:13 says, "It is God who works in you both to *will* and to *do* His good pleasure." He gives us the will, or *desire*, to please Him, and then He gives us the *ability*. I prayed that God would give me the desire to do this, and He has been answering that prayer by giving me the desire to be healthy and work out regularly.

I also pray almost daily that He will make me a woman of moderation. He loves to answer prayers like that! It has become apparent too that we don't make our health care decisions in just doctors' offices or hospitals alone. We first make them in grocery stores and restaurants. My deepest needs can either take me to food or take me to God. But God desires and is able to bring true healing. I cannot deliver myself; I've already tried. However, a great truth that encourages me is the fact that His Word states that self-control is not an act of the will but rather a fruit of the Holy Spirit for which we can pray.

I remember shopping at Wal-Mart during my lunch hour one afternoon and resisting the urge to buy chocolate Teddy Grahams. At the time, these little cookies were a great temptation since I could eat nearly an entire box in one sitting. I managed to leave the store without buying any only to turn around before I reached my car to head back in and give in to that temptation. I stopped in my tracks as I recalled the verse I'd learned the day before, "All things are lawful for me, but I will not be mastered by anything." (1 Corinthians 6:12) I repeated that verse out loud as I fought the Teddy Graham war.

The Living Bible puts it this way:

> "I can do anything I want to if Christ has not said no, but some of these things aren't good for me. Even if I am allowed to do them, I'll refuse to if I think they might get such a grip on me that I can't easily stop when I want to. For instance, take the matter of eating. God has given us an appetite for food and stomachs to digest it. But that doesn't mean we should eat more than we need. Don't think of eating as important because someday God will do away with both stomachs and

food."

The popular saying, "Nothing tastes as good as skinny feels," seems better stated, "Nothing tastes as good as healthy feels." The goal of being skinny is not my main focus. Life is a valuable gift from a loving God. I strive to honor the Giver of the gift of health with the way that I treat that gift, my body. Romans 14:20 has become one of my favorites: "Do not destroy the work of God for the sake of food."

Surely this struggle with overeating and obesity has reached epidemic proportions in the U.S. in the last several decades. I know I'm in good company when I chide myself not to look to food for answers to emotional pain. They are not there. In fact, food causes *more* emotional pain. Restraint means that if I am going to live in victory, I have to learn to say "no" every single day, more than once a day. Our pastor, Steve, once remarked, "One of the main things we struggle with is learning to balance the pleasures and blessings of life." "So whether you eat or drink or whatever you do, do it all for the glory of God." (1 Corinthians 10:31)

CHAPTER 12

God Will Direct Your Ministry

"He who refreshes others will himself be refreshed."
~ Proverbs 11:25

AIDEE

THE WORLD IS changed by your example, not your opinion. It was time to add action to my convictions. After receiving Christ as my Savior, I had a strong desire to share this new freedom with others. I've heard it said that a life *contemplating* the blessings of Christ becomes a life *acting* the love of Christ. God was alive and well in my life, He had set me free, and I wanted to shout it from the rooftops. When faced with the needs of others, doing nothing just didn't feel right. I longed to be used by God to be a blessing to others.

We were still attending the Catholic Church, and I had very little direction or resources. I was listening to a call-in radio program one day where the guest speaker was talking about God using us to minister to others. For the first (and last!) time in my life, I mustered up the courage to call in. When I asked where I should start serving, the speaker wisely told me that God would direct my ministry. If God was in it, all I had to do was keep my eyes on Him and be willing to be used, and He would lead people to me. I could do that! It's been my motto ever since to keep my eyes on Him with hands open to what He puts into them. Since that time, I have never lacked ministry opportunities.

The first person the Lord put in my life to mentor was Aidee. The Big Brothers Big Sisters of Delaware was looking for Big Sisters to spend time with girls who needed love and direction. The mission of Big Sisters is to "provide children facing adversity with strong and enduring professionally supported one-to-one relationships that change their lives for the better, forever." Although I was only 24 years old, and didn't have much life experience, God had changed my life forever for the better so sharing that experience with Aidee was a natural overflow of the joy I was now experiencing. I had so much new-found joy in my life, I was happy to have it splash out onto others.

After going through the background checks, interviews, and training Big Sisters required, I was matched with Aidee, a ten-year-old little girl whose father had recently committed suicide. Aidee was the quietest young lady I've ever met, shy and withdrawn. I found it challenging to spend time with Aidee because most of our conversations were a one way street. Although later in our relationship Dan and I would take Aidee to the Philadelphia Zoo and other outings, Big Sisters emphasized initially spending time together and getting to know one another during the normal activities of daily living. Aidee and I played with the dog, went for long walks, planted flowers, read books, decorated the Christmas tree: things most parents and kids do together. After getting together once a week for several weeks, I found Aidee to be almost as quiet as when we first met. Although I would now catch a flicker of a smile on her face when I joked, and she warmed up to my generous supply of hugs, I began to wonder if Aidee disliked me or if she secretly wished she had been given a different Big Sister. I've found that just because an activity may be divinely orchestrated, that doesn't stop the Enemy from making us question ourselves or feel defeated in the process.

One day my fears were relieved when I dropped Aidee off at her home. After Aidee left the room, her mom told me how Aidee loved our times together and that she couldn't stop talking about me and the things we did together. I was astonished! Her mom relayed minute details of activities we had done together and Aidee's comments about all of them. Aidee was a wounded child with a tender heart. Losing her dad to suicide at such a young age, she had experienced more pain than I can comprehend. Aidee was soaking everything in; I just had to be content with the fact that I was sowing seeds that might blossom later in her life. When the program ended, Aidee and her mom moved, and we lost touch with each other. I often wonder what became of Aidee and hope to meet her again in heaven one day. Years later, I drew on my experiences with Aidee when I worked with orphans in the Central African Republic. Like Aidee, those were deeply wounded children, many of whom were stoic on the outside, but I could be sure that on the inside they were drinking in the love we lavished on them.

It's not just the orphans of the world who have scars. We all have them. One of my favorite poems is about our One and Only and the scars we all must bear.

Hast Thou No Scar?
by Amy Carmichael

Hast thou no scar?
No hidden scar on foot, or side, or hand?
I hear thee sung as mighty in the land,
I hear them hail thy bright ascendant star,
Hast thou no scar?

Hast thou no wound?
Yet, I was wounded by the archers, spent.
Leaned me against the tree to die, and rent
By ravening beasts that compassed me, I swooned:
Hast thou no wound?

No wound? No scar?
Yet as the Master shall the servant be,

And, pierced are the feet that follow Me;
But thine are whole; Can he have followed far
Who has no wound nor scar?

CHAPTER 13

Women in Crisis Pregnancies

"Faith is like lenses in a pair of glasses: they don't change circumstances, just perspective."
~ Chuck Swindoll

IN 1986, THE Lord called me to minister with Crisis Pregnancy Center, an abortion alternative service that offers help to women in crisis pregnancies. In retrospect, the Lord had been softening my heart to this call for many years.

When the Supreme Court legalized abortion in 1973, I was only 19 years old and worked as a medical transcriptionist in the typing pool of a private hospital in Wilkes-Barre, PA. Growing up in the Catholic Church, I had a natural bent toward being pro-life but had never been impacted personally with the issue of abortion. As a transcriber of surgical procedures, I began to see a new procedure dictated in the pool of operative reports. I routinely typed D&C's, which stands for dilatation and curettage, a relatively routine procedure often performed after a woman experiences miscarriage. This new procedure was listed as a D&E: dilatation and evacuation. As I listened to the surgeon dictating the report, it became apparent to me that he was describing an abortion procedure. It was quite shocking and it saddened me to hear graphic details of how the fetus was removed using a curette (a sharp instrument used to scrape a woman's uterus) and then evacuated or extracted.

I vividly remember the moment when it occurred to me that as a health care worker, I was now part of the legalized abortion system. Although I knew that my involvement was remote, and was in no way promoting abortions, I quickly came to the conclusion that my conscience would not allow me to take any part in something which I so strongly disapproved. The words of Martin Luther rang in my ears, "You are not only responsible for what you say, but also for what you do not say." I went to my supervisor and told her that I would not transcribe abortion procedures. Although she seemed surprised by my strong stand, she distributed those procedures to other employees who were willing to type them.

The pro-life/pro-choice debate continued to rage on, dividing our country as it still does to this day. In some ways, the '70s and '80s seemed more volatile than ever, with demonstrations on both sides leading to arrests, bombings of abortion clinics, and even the appalling murder of a physician who performed abortions. I was very happy to quietly "fly under the radar" with pro-life views but never intended to go any further than that. However, God had something else in mind.

One day in 1986 I engaged in an intimate and candid conversation with a lady in her late 60s. That conversation would change the course of my life. This was a lady who was always responsive and interested when I talked about God. I think she reveled in the joy that she saw in me even though she felt that it was something she could never enjoy. Her life was riddled with anxiety and worry, and it broke my heart to see her in such bondage, especially since I myself had been set free. She often spoke of having experienced a traumatic miscarriage years earlier that she never seemed to be able to get over.

Finally, our long talk about God led me to ask her, "If you died and stood before God tonight and He asked you why He should let you in heaven, what would you say?" I expected her to say that she was a good person and that's why she would be allowed to go to heaven. I sat astounded when she answered, "I am not going to heaven when I die. I have done something that can never be forgiven." She proceeded to tell me that although she told others that she lost her baby through miscarriage, it was actually an abortion she had experienced years earlier. I was shocked. This was something only she, the father of her baby, and the abortionist knew. She had felt that she had no other options and was pressured to have the procedure performed long before abortion was legalized.

I reeled as I imagined what horrors she must have endured by having such a procedure performed by a back-alley abortionist. I was stunned and filled with compassion now as I saw this lady in a different light than I ever had before. It was a decision she regretted the rest of her life, especially after she had children and realized the great joy of being a mother. This explained why she still cried profusely when she spoke of losing that baby. The guilt and regret she carried all these years was tremendous. This was why she didn't attend church and why she seemed nervous and cried constantly on the few occasions when she entered a church for a wedding or funeral. This was why she was so overprotective of her living children. She had never forgiven herself for killing her unborn child, the choice she had felt was her only option at the time.

I thank God to this day that He gave me the grace to respond quickly and in love. I wept with her. With great compassion, I told her there was nothing that she had done that was any worse than the least of the sins I had ever committed. God's grace was needed in my life in the same way it was in hers. I immediately told her that Christ died for all of her sins - including abortion. I shared the gospel with her as I assured her that no sin was unforgivable and that Jesus bore that sin on the cross, as well as all the others she or I had ever committed. I urged her to ask God for forgiveness and to get on with the business of forgiving herself.

The spell was broken, however, when her phone rang, and the moment was lost forever. After answering the phone and briefly chatting with the caller, the mood was different, and this lady was uncomfortable going back to our discussion. A year later when she became seriously ill, I wanted to be sure she understood the forgiveness that was offered through Christ. Just a few months before she passed away, I made a special trip to see her to once again revisit that subject.

Although I shared with her the Good News of Christ's death and resurrection one more time, I never had the pleasure of seeing her come to Christ. My hope is that she did, and I will be overjoyed to see her in heaven.

Soon after this fateful event took place, I came across a startling ad in a popular ladies magazine. The ad read, "If you choose to have an abortion, we stand behind you." Pictured was a young lady standing with about 20 men and women fanned out behind her, people representing judges, doctors, nurses, lawyers, ministers, police officers and office workers. I thought to myself, "Where are the ads that say, 'If you choose NOT to abort, we stand behind you.'?"

Although contemporary society generally supports women who are single parents and at times our government has even made it financially beneficial to be a single mother, in 1986 when a girl or woman was in a crisis pregnancy, it was considered a shameful situation and often people abandoned her or looked the other way. At that time, a girl who found herself pregnant and unwed could secretly have an abortion and never lose face, while the girl who chose to give life to her child suffered contempt from society as well as the extreme stress of enduring the pregnancy and then raising her child, often alone and in a financial disaster. God was building in me a deep sense of love and concern for all women, including both the ones who chose abortion – and often needed emotional and spiritual healing from that decision – *and* the ones who chose life for their unborn children.

The final straw that God used to push me into action was a film that was shown at Grace Church during Sunday School about a month later. The film was called *Silent Scream*, a gripping and powerful portrayal of the "silent scream" of a life that is ended when an abortion is performed. I was moved to tears. When the movie ended, there was a plea for women to volunteer their time at the Augusta Crisis Pregnancy Center (CPC). Although there is currently an Aiken CPC, the closest CPC at that time was the one in Augusta. I didn't have to think twice. I felt compelled to act, and I signed up for their volunteer training.

I couldn't be there for my friend so many years ago, to be there to help her through her unwanted pregnancy or to love on her after she made that ill-fated decision. But I could be there for other women in her situation, and I knew that was God's call on my life. After several weeks of training I was asked to be a hotline volunteer. A hotline counselor would be on call once a week for a 24 hour period manning the CPC crisis hotline. This was long before cell phones, so that meant staying home and being available to answer any call morning or night for a 24-hour period once a week. How could I say yes to such a formidable task, especially while taking care of Aaron and Ashley, then aged one and four? Our home was noisy and busy and chaotic, and I was supposed to take urgent calls from girls in crisis at any time of the day and be expected to give intelligent, meaningful advice and counsel? It seemed impossible.

When I shared those fears with our volunteer coordinator, she told me that I simply needed to trust God and let Him be in charge of those worries. Was my God too small for this? Certainly not. It was another one of those times that I lived the truth of Philippians 2:13: "For it is God who works in you, both to will and to work for His good pleasure." If it was God's will for me to do this, then it was up to Him to enable me.

I served as a hotline counselor for almost seven years, and I can honestly say I don't remember ever having to miss a phone call due to problems with the kids. On the days I was on call, I kept an extra toy or two on hand that were only brought out when Mommy was on a "special call." It was uncanny to watch how God seemed to miraculously soften the children on those days as they played quietly while I took those brief calls.

CHAPTER 14

Shepherding Unwed Mothers

Bear not a single care thyself,
One is too much for thee.
The work is Mine and Mine alone,
Thy work, to rest in Me.
- Missionary Hudson Taylor

I HAD BEEN a hotline counselor for a number of years when I received a very special call late one night. It was perhaps 11:00 p.m., and the kids and Dan were fast asleep upstairs. I was startled when the phone rang that late. I was again startled when the man on the other end announced that he was a police officer. He had called the number for the Pregnancy Center Hotline because he had a girl in a crisis pregnancy. He relayed to me that sitting across from him in the police station was a girl named Angela. She was 16 and pregnant. Her boyfriend and parents wanted her to abort, and when she refused, the conflict that ensued led her to run away from home several weeks earlier. She was a drifter, having dropped out of school and staying with friends whose lives were in just as much chaos as hers. That night, Angela had been sleeping on the couch of a friend whose boyfriend was using drugs, and after he got high he had become abusive. Angela ran for her life, literally barefoot and pregnant, and finally ran to the police station because she had nowhere left to go. Now the police were calling me for help.

The officer said that although he had arranged for Angela to be transported the following morning to a home for unwed mothers in Charleston, SC, there was nowhere for her to spend the night. If she stayed at the station she would have to sleep in a chair. I told him I would see what I could do and promised to call him back with an answer.

What ensued was two hours of conversations between me and Susan Swanson, the Augusta CPC director, as well as representatives from any agency who could possibly help. At that time, The Aiken Salvation Army Shelter and The Home for Abused Women were not in existence. Susan Swanson was the first one to suggest out loud what I felt was being whispered to me on the inside...are you willing to open your home to Angela? I thought of all the reasons this was risky and insane. I didn't know this girl at all, and the little I knew about her was alarming. She had obviously made some very bad choices, was at least living with people who drank and did drugs and may well have been using drugs herself. There was also the risk of disease, including AIDS. She was at the end of her rope. What if she decided to abuse my good will and steal from us, or worse, hurt one of my children? What if her volatile friend found out where she was and showed up at my house?

As the evening wore on, and we became more desperate for an answer, I quietly began asking God if His will was for me to open my home to her. The Lord taught me long ago that my husband and I are a team and that no big decision should be made without his input. I went upstairs and awakened Dan. After explaining the situation to him, he agreed to let Angela stay at our house. His only request was that I lock the door to the kids' bedroom to make sure they were safe if Angela should have any ulterior motives.

It was around 2:00 a.m. when the squad car pulled up in front of our house. Since we didn't have a guest room at the time, I prepared the sofa bed in our play room as Angela's bed. With a knot in my stomach and bracing myself for a rough-and-tumble juvenile delinquent to be brought to my door, I anxiously stood on the porch. I was shocked when out of the squad car stepped an adorable young girl, diminutive in size, shy and quiet in appearance. She walked barefoot up my sidewalk wearing only pajamas. The officer placed a blanket over her shoulders, and it seemed to swallow her. I welcomed her and showed her to "her room."

To my surprise and delight what Angela wanted more than a good night's sleep was a sympathetic, listening ear. I could be that! The Lord had already given me so much love and empathy for this young girl that she easily opened up about the events that led her to this night. I was surprised to find that she was from a middle class family and had attended private school. It was only recently that her life had derailed, and she was determined to have this baby and get her life back on track again. We talked until the sun came up. In just a few hours Susan Swanson would pick her up and take her to the Maternity Home in Charleston. I insisted that she get a few hours of sleep.

While Angela slept I realized that this girl literally didn't have a thing to her name, not even a pair of clean underwear or clothes to wear. I had long since passed along my maternity clothes to friends and therefore had nothing that would fit her. I called my best good friend and neighbor, Sheilah, and asked her to come to our aid. She was thrilled to help out and soon my mailbox was stuffed with a maternity outfit complete with brand new undies and all. After Angela was refreshed with a few hours of sleep, a shower, clean clothing, and a nourishing breakfast, it was time to say our goodbyes. I showered her with hugs and words of encouragement. Angela thanked me profusely, and we said our farewells as I entrusted her to the person who would accompany her to the next step in her journey.

Due to privacy laws and the nature of maternity homes, like so many of the people whom God has placed in my life, I never saw Angela again nor do I know "the rest of the story." It is enough to know that I answered the call God put on my life that night, and I was blessed abundantly for it by the few hours I got to spend with a sweet girl named Angela.

My positive experience with Angela led Dan and me to agree to go through the interview and training process to become shepherding parents through Crisis Pregnancy Center (CPC). A shepherding home was one in which an unwed mother, in need of housing, would live until she delivered her baby. After initial interviews with the client, CPC would place the girl in a home they felt was compatible.

Our home became one of the five homes available in Aiken. The center provided an informal contract between the shepherding home and the client. Very clear parameters were defined. If either side broke the contract, the young lady would be asked to move out. We decided since we had a young daughter and son, Ashley and Aaron, at home who needed their own rooms, we would only offer our home for the girls to live in on a "part time" basis. Mostly they stayed with us on the weekends, when we could let them have Ashley's room and put Ashley on the couch without leaving Ashley sleep deprived for school. We assumed complete responsibility for each girl and treated her like a daughter: cooking her meals, washing her clothes, giving her rides, and including her in family activities. Of course, we also expected each girl to contribute to the running of the home, just like we did with our children.

Madeleine was the first young lady the Lord brought us. She was 19 years old, pregnant, and had been abandoned by her boyfriend and family. Scott, the father of the baby, had become emotionally and even physically abusive and finally left Madeleine when he realized she wasn't going to abort. Madeleine actually had quite a large family living in Aiken, but there was a lot of dysfunction in the family, and her parents were not supportive of her.

When Madeleine came to live with us, she had already decided that she was not prepared to be a mother but was planning to place her baby for adoption. Madeleine never referred to the baby at all. It was like she totally ignored the fact that she was pregnant. Apparently it was her way of detaching herself from a baby she knew she wasn't going to keep and didn't want to bond with anyway.

Madeleine was relatively easy to live with, and we got along very well. As a matter of fact, both she and Amy, the next girl who lived with us, preferred our home to their "full time" shepherding home, and both asked to stay with us on a full time basis. In retrospect, even though it was very hard at the time, I am so grateful I had the courage to say "no" to those requests and to keep my own children as my priority. I hope it set an example to my children that even though Daddy and I were ministering to other people, and even letting them live in our home, our children were our priority and their needs were paramount.

Madeleine asked me to be her birth coach and wanted me in the delivery room with her. I was honored and agreed. It was an experience I will never forget. Tuesday, November 10, 1992 began with a phone call from Kathy, the mom in the other shepherding home where Madeline spent most days. Kathy had four children, so I assumed she would recognize the signs of active labor should Madeleine be with her at the time she started labor. What I didn't know was that each of Kathy's four births had been scheduled Caesarean births, and she had never experienced a normal, active labor. Therefore, neither she nor Madeleine recognized Madeleine's labor until it was almost too late to get her to the hospital.

When Kathy called, she asked me to talk to Madeleine because Madeleine had some cramps, was being "difficult," had gone to bed, and wouldn't come out of her room. When I questioned Kathy some more, I realized Madeleine was well into active labor but no one realized it. I dropped everything and drove to the house. When I went into Madeline's room, she was curled up on the bed in a fetal position moaning in pain. I told her we needed to leave for the ER. Crying, she refused. She was paralyzed by pain and fear and wasn't thinking rationally.

Madeleine had not packed a suitcase for the hospital as she had been told to do weeks earlier. I finally got her out of bed and watched in distress as she shuffled around the room, crying and trying to pack, but not even able to focus enough to get anything accomplished. I could see that I had to get her to hospital and decided I would take her belongings to her later. As we drove to the hospital 30 minutes away, Madeleine lay in the back seat moaning and crying. Fearful that we wouldn't arrive to the hospital in time, I sat in the front seat driving and secretly moaning and praying.

Thankfully, we made it to St. Joseph's Hospital just in time for them to give her an epidural before delivery, which happened soon after that. What an honor it was to physically help hold Madeleine as she delivered the baby and to be the only one in the room other than the doctor and nurse. After pushing for over an hour, with one strong, final push, Madeleine gave birth to little Christina. She was beautiful and perfect in every way, with thick, dark hair and beautiful skin tone.

Madeleine remained detached from her baby and, per her request, chose to not even hold her. With quiet resolve and no emotion, the nurse wrapped the baby in a blanket and whisked her away.

Madeleine displayed a sense of relief but absolutely no maternal emotions. It was all very calm and quiet and sterile, so unlike the births of my own babies and grandchildren, which were fabulous times of euphoria and celebration. I was reminded again of the differences between God's best and anything else. God's perfect plan is to have each child born into a loving home with a father and mother who are bound by a marriage covenant. Although the Lord is merciful to mothers who fall outside of that plan, anything less than that misses the mark for God's best for us.

I was very impressed with how Madeleine's obstetrician conducted himself. He was attentive and considerate throughout Madeleine's labor. As soon as the baby was carried out of the room, the doctor came to Madeleine's side and held her hand. Looking intently into her eyes, he said in a very deliberate tone, "Madeleine, what you've done here is a wonderful thing. You have given life." It was a touching demonstration of compassion and recognition of the fact that this young mother, in spite of her own shortcomings and fears, chose life. This new life, named Christina, was adopted by a wonderful Christian family chosen by Madeleine.

I stayed with Madeleine for the remainder of the evening and drove home at 3:00 a.m. I found out the next day that the baby's father, Scott, showed up at the hospital shortly after I left. He wanted to renew his relationship with Madeleine now that the baby was out of the picture. Madeleine, being vulnerable and needy, renewed her relationship with him.

A few months later when Scott and Madeleine decided they wanted to get married, they asked our pastor if he would marry them. Thankfully, he declined. I had to find a way to show Madeleine that this young man was not someone she should spend the rest of her life with. I suspected that he was physically abusing her, but she denied it.

Pastor Steve wisely suggested that Dan and I get together with them for a little premarital counseling involving a game. Steve gave us the game which was very similar to The Newlywed Game but with even more intimate, probing questions which were designed to help partners learn about each other's character and values. It only took a couple of weeks for Scott to expose himself for what he was: an immature, arrogant and selfish young man who was mistreating Madeleine. We could have argued with Madeleine all day long about Scott's pros and cons, and she would have fallen into a defensive posture. But with this game, Madeleine witnessed with her own eyes, and heard with her own ears, his lack of honor and morals. I watched a growing sense of astonishment, and ultimately disgust in Madeleine's face, as week after week Scott revealed his true inner self. She finally stopped making excuses for him and admitted he had been physically abusing her. Much to our relief, she called the wedding off and they broke up.

For the next several years, Madeleine and I kept in touch. She always called me on Mother's Day and expressed her gratitude. But we lost touch, and I have not heard from her in several years and have been unable to locate her. I still think of Madeleine often, say a prayer, and hope she is doing well.

The next young lady who came into our lives was 17-year-old Amy. Amy also came from a home in Aiken. She lived with her mother, who was losing control of Amy. Once again, there was much turmoil in their home, and her mother wanted Amy out. Amy was staying out all night and sleeping during the day, refusing to go to school, and generally being difficult. I recall the pregnancy center director telling me that if I could get Amy's nights and days straightened out, that in itself would be a big accomplishment.

I agreed to pick Amy up at the center. I'm not sure what I expected to see after hearing about this "pregnant problem child," but Amy didn't fit the role. She was blonde and perky and adorable. I liked Amy instantly. She had a very outgoing nature and infectious personality. We hit it off immediately. I brought her home and that night, after dinner, Amy and I sat cross legged on the floor in front of our fireplace. As we stared at the fire, Amy spoke openly about the trying times in her life that led her to that point. At 16, Amy had been through a lot, and God gave me a great amount of compassion for her. We sat and talked and cried together, and God knit our hearts to one another.

Amy had a sister who had struggles of her own, but the two of them were emotionally very close. Later that evening when Amy's sister called, Amy didn't try to hide her part of the conversation.

"Hey, Sis, guess what this family did at dinner? They actually sat down at the table together and held hands and prayed. It's just like *Leave it to Beaver* around here!"

I laughed out loud and later asked Amy what the custom was in her home when it came to meals.

"Well, first of all, we never pray. And whenever anybody wants to eat, they just eat. We don't ever sit down together at the same time."

"What about at Thanksgiving or Christmas?" I asked.

"Same thing. Holidays are just another day at our house."

Even though Amy had lots of emotional baggage, I found her to be an absolute delight to have around the house. The kids loved her, and so did Dan and I. She had a great sense of humor and cracked jokes and laughed easily. Unlike Madeleine, Amy was looking forward to the birth of her baby and planned to keep the child and raise it. Amy's days and nights being mixed up didn't remain a problem for very long. At my insistence, Amy got up early in the morning, like it or not. After a day or two of shuffling around the house half asleep, with me keeping her busy with things to do, she was happy to go to bed at a decent time. Amy's custom at home was to crawl out of her bedroom window to spend the night partying. She knew if she tried that with us she would be kicked out of our house, which would be the end of the road for her. No problems there.

Although we respected the girls' privacy and didn't let our kids in on the intimate details of their lives, there were instances that became good teaching tools. For example, while Amy was living with us she had to perform community service activities for a legal misdemeanor. One morning when Amy was sleepily getting out of bed to serve her sentence, Ashley commented on how wonderful it was that Amy was helping people. Fearing that Ashley was failing to realize that Amy was only in this situation to begin with because she had broken the law, I gently explained to Ashley that the good deeds Amy was performing were ordered by the court. It was the perfect opportunity for me to explain cause and effect and the consequences of our actions.

Several months later, Amy delivered a precious baby boy named Zain, whom she loved and cared for tenderly. After seeing each other a few times after Zain was born, Amy and I lost touch with one another.

Fourteen years passed before we would meet again at the high school graduation of a mutual friend. I was thrilled to see Amy, but what she told me thrilled me even more. Amy had come to Christ! She proudly introduced me once again to Zain, now almost as tall as me. She was accompanied by her other young son and daughter and told me that she was married to a wonderful Christian who loved her.

"Oh Miss Peggy, I have everything you ever wanted for me!" she exclaimed. I have seen Amy and her family many times since then, since her husband and a mutual friend are in a Christian band we frequently go to see. What a gift that God has let me see "the rest of the story," and how He redeemed Amy's life! As a matter of fact, a couple of years ago, Amy and I were asked to speak at a conference for pastors and Christian leaders in the Augusta community. What a joy it was to stand next to Amy as we told of God's love and ability to make beauty out of ashes and to make all things new.

Dan and I prayed often about the influence these young ladies were having on our children. A few acquaintances even questioned the wisdom of exposing our kids to such drama. Weren't we worried about things like venereal disease, AIDS, or the fact that the lifestyle of an unwed mother might appear attractive to our impressionable young kids? These issues, and many more, were risks I had already considered and prayed about. Crisis Pregnancy Centers had designed a very specific code of conduct for the protection of their pregnant clients as well as the Shepherding Homes which were signed by all parties. We were very vigilant and intentional about our decisions, which were bathed in prayer, as we trusted God to lead us.

It's now been over 20 years since Amy left our home. I can look back and thank the Lord for His wisdom and direction in accomplishing what He had planned. Dan and I had our faith stretched, we learned a lot, and each of the girls received plenty of love and care during their time of need. Ashley and Aaron learned firsthand that the "sixteen and pregnant" lifestyle was not at all glamorous. On the contrary, although they had tons of compassion and genuine love for Madeleine and Amy, they knew better than anyone that there were consequences to premarital sex. It may have been one of the best commercials ever to underscore what they were learning at home: that abstinence before marriage is God's perfect plan.

I am pleased to say that Ashley has become quite a pro-life advocate in her own right. She was actively involved with Dayspring, the Crisis Pregnancy Center in Columbia, SC, when she lived there. She has spent a great deal of time educating herself about the miracle of life, which has led her to be passionate and supportive of organizations such as Save the Storks. I can't help but believe that God was planting seeds of ministry in Ashley when she was a young girl willingly giving up her room and sharing her parents with girls in need. Now she is sharing her life with girls in need.

CHAPTER 15

Learning to Forgive

"The cup that is full of sweet water cannot spill bitter-tasting drops however sharply it is knocked."
- Amy Carmichael

THE ABOVE QUOTE from Amy Carmichael is one that has touched me deeply and convicted me greatly. It is with fear and trembling that I even begin to approach the subject of forgiveness because I am still a life-long student in the school of forgiveness. I've just begun to feel around the edges of these truths. What propels me down the road of forgiveness is the healing I receive and can give to some of the other broken people of the world. I have never met another human being who hasn't had to forgive someone, or many others, of something.

Perhaps the One we all struggle to forgive is God. Let's face it. When we encounter suffering, our first instinct is to escape or to try to avoid suffering altogether. When we cannot, we blame God for allowing such pain in our lives. Ultimately, if we believe God is completely sovereign, then we are faced with accepting that suffering is filtered through the hands of a loving God. One of my favorite excerpts from *Hinds' Feet on High Places* addresses the fact that suffering may come from another person or situation outside of our control, but ultimately it is allowed by God and intended for our benefit. In the story, a lone flower named Forgiveness growing in the crevice of a rock says:

> "I was separated from all my companions, exiled from home, carried here and imprisoned in this rock. It was not my choice but the work of others who, when they had dropped me here, went away and left me to bear the results of what they had done. I have borne, and have not fainted, and I have not ceased to love, and Love [Christ] has helped me push through the crack in the rock until I could look right out onto my Love the sun [Son] Himself. See now! There is nothing whatever between my Love and my heart, nothing around to distract me from Him. He shines on me and makes me to rejoice, and He has atoned to me for all that was taken from me and done against me. There is no flower in all the world more blessed and more satisfied than I, for I look up to Him as a weaned child and say, 'Whom have I in heaven but Thee, and there is none upon earth that I desire but Thee.'"

Luke 6:37 commands us to "Forgive, and you will be forgiven." As a Christian, I have embraced the fact that God allowed His one and only Son to die on the cross in payment for my sin. That makes me a trophy of His abundant grace. If I am unwilling to forgive another person and work on that relationship, then I am saying that my standards are higher than God's. I am a blood-bought sinner, a trophy of the grace of God in my life. The grace of the cross was extended to me, an undeserving sinner. Do I extend that same grace to someone who has deeply wounded me?

I don't do it because they deserve it. I do it because of Jesus and what He did for me. I am learning that when I hold on to anger and refuse to forgive, I remain tied to the offender and to the past. I want to be liberated from the past. God's grace is a generous grace. Do I lavish on others the Christ-like grace that was lavished on me? God has been a giver of grace to me. Am I a grace giver?

Who can bring peace unless they have held their own peace? It is my calling to experience unjust hurt in my life. This is not merely a rule to follow. It is a grace to be received. This is a miracle to be experienced. 1 Peter 2:18-25 says it is my vocation to be mistreated and not to become bitter:

> "Servants, be submissive to your masters with all fear, not only to the good and gentle, but also to the harsh. For this is commendable, if because of conscience toward God one endures grief, suffering wrongfully.

For what credit is it if, when you are beaten for your faults, you take it patiently? But when you do well and suffer, if you take it patiently, this is commendable before God. For to this you were called, because Christ also suffered for us, leaving us an example, that you should follow His steps: 'Who committed no sin, Nor was deceit found in His mouth; who, when He was reviled, did not revile in return; when He suffered, He did not threaten, but committed Himself to Him who judges righteously; who Himself bore our sins in His own body on the tree, that we, having died to sins, might live for righteousness – by whose stripes you were healed. For you were like sheep going astray, but have now returned to the Shepherd and Overseer of your souls."

I heard it said once that if you see a marriage that has gone the distance, you know it's made up of two people who are good forgivers. No other relationship is as intimate and intense as husband and wife. Such intimacy and intensity brings about the greatest potential for us to cause each other pain, and this will require the act of forgiveness. Let's face it: we are all by nature very selfish. We want what we want and we want it now. "The thing in us that reacts so sharply to another's selfishness and pride is simply our own selfishness and pride." (Roy Hession, *Calvary Road*)

In his book entitled *Total Forgiveness*, R. T. Kendall puts it this way: "Total forgiveness is painful. It hurts to think the person is getting away with what they did. But when we fully accept in our hearts that they will be blessed without any consequences for their wrong, we cross over into a supernatural realm. We begin to be a little more like Jesus, to change into the image of Christ."

On the contrary, a lack of forgiveness leads to bitterness. Some people have a real problem with bitterness, and they don't even know what the problem is. Of one thing I am certain: lack of forgiveness will cost you. Just like dogs can sense fear in people, people sense bitterness in one another. They don't even always know what they are sensing, but they don't do business with it. They don't want to be friends with it or ask it out on a second date. They don't stay married to it forever. People stay away from people in whom they sense bitterness. Bitterness will kill you.

Like any other marriage, mine has been a marriage where forgiveness has been in great demand. Neither of us were believers when we married, and both of us came from homes where, to put it mildly, marital discord was the norm. I had wrong thinking, and wrong thinking brings about wrong living. I had need of much forgiveness. Suffice it to say that we came into our union with poor communication and coping skills. We were ripe for turmoil. God cannot pour His riches into hands that are already full of unforgiveness, anger, and bitterness, and I would come to learn I had much to let go of before I was ready to receive all his goodness. Looking back and reliving the past filled me with anger and stole the energy I needed to move forward.

The Lord began teaching me what a weighty responsibility my husband and I have as the matriarch and patriarch of our family. When our lives are connected, our behavior can have unintended consequences for other people; what I sow, you reap.

The book of Joshua demonstrates this principle in the story of Achan. God gives the Israelites a great victory at Jericho, but He specifically commands his people not to take any of the spoils of Jericho. "And you, by all means keep yourselves from the accursed things lest you become accursed when you take of the accursed things, *and make the camp of Israel a curse and trouble it.*" (Joshua 6:18, emphasis mine) But an Israelite named Achan disregards this command and takes some of the accursed things. More than 36 people in the camp die as a result of Achan's disobedience.

God was teaching me that habitual sin committed by the mom or dad impacts the entire family. The anger issues Dan and I faced were affecting our entire camp: our family. Joshua 24:14-15 were brought to life for me at that time:

> "So revere Jehovah and serve Him in sincerity and truth. Put away forever the idols your ancestors worshiped when they lived beyond the Euphrates River and in Egypt. Worship the Lord alone. But if you are unwilling to obey the Lord, then decide today whom you will obey. Will it be the gods of your ancestors beyond the

Euphrates or the gods of the Amorites here in this land? But as for me and my family, we will serve the Lord."

Would Dan and I repeat the failures of our parents or choose to let God begin a new work in our family? My choices would impact those coming behind me. The good news is that although we are all products of our past, we don't have to be prisoners of it. I needed to empathize with my parents (my ancestors) and begin to forgive some poor choices they made. After all, I know how much I want to avoid these patterns, but even I find myself easily slipping back into negative behavior.

"Love keeps no record of wrongs." (1 Corinthians 13:5) Love doesn't erase our memories. It is actually a demonstration of greater grace when we are fully aware of what occurred and we still choose to forgive. I can choose not to remember. Total forgiveness must go on and on. Some days will be harder than others.

I'm often tempted to believe that long-held sin or disturbing situations that have been ingrained for years will never change. It's at those times I recall what the Lord did for our marriage in 2008. The Lord was teaching me that my background is not my destiny. On the first Sunday of the new year, Pastor Steve built a sermon around Isaiah 43:18-19, which says, "Do not remember the former things, nor consider the things of old. Behold, I will do a new thing."

When he taught from this passage, the Lord stirred my heart with a sense that He wanted to do a new work in my life, specifically in my marriage. Boy, was I ever right about that! Although Dan and I have spent over 40 years learning to love the way the Lord intended, I look back to that Sunday in 2008 as the beginning of a true transformation in our lives through His grace.

I have witnessed marriages that had far worse problems than ours, and were even on the brink of divorce, that managed not only to survive but to thrive and come back better than ever. The changes I've seen in myself and my marriage have left me with a deep-seated belief that no marriage is beyond reach for God to heal.

When we go through tumultuous times in our early years, we can be left with crippling regret. God is teaching me to cast my care on Him and to rely on Him to restore the wasted years. "I will restore to you the years that the swarming locust has eaten," promises God in Joel 2:25. I find that the more conscious I am of the work the Lord has yet to do in me, the less conscious I am of the work He has yet to do in others.

I have seen the Lord fulfill that promise in regards to our vacations and travel as a couple and as a family. Like many families, traveling together and vacations seemed to be some of our greatest triggers for conflict. By God's grace, I fought the temptation to give up and allow our past habits and failures to conquer us. God was teaching me that a person who lives in the past doesn't live at all. He was shouting to me, "Let the past be the past at last!"

Starting in 1999, the Lord began giving us amazing opportunities to travel. Then in 2008 when Aaron began working for American Eagle Airlines, and we received flight benefits, the opportunities abounded. Would I embrace them as a gift from God and expect great things from Him by faith, or would I let memories of the past defeat me and leave me afraid to step out in faith? After all, "Love keeps no record of wrongs," right? I was once again learning to choose obedience over feelings. I knew that when we are dependent upon God, we have His strength. Would I apply those lessons to these new challenges? These travels put to the test some of the coping techniques Dan and I were learning in counseling and taught us to depend on the promises of God. I am delighted and humbled to say that what has followed have been many years of amazing travels that have built new and wonderful memories which have more than made up for the "years the locust had eaten."

Ultimately, God is sovereign. If I truly believe that, then I know that even the pain He has allowed others to cause in my life has been filtered through His omnipotent hands. In some ways, if it were not for injustices and pain, I might never have run into the arms of Christ. This is very aptly portrayed in the new version of Cinderella which Disney released in 2015. A favorite line in that movie comes as Ella is treated dreadfully by her stepsisters. As a result, she furiously rides her horse into the forest and there meets the prince. "Perhaps it was just as well Ella's stepsisters were cruel, for had she not run to the forest, she might never have met the prince." We are Cinderella, Christ is our prince.

I'm beginning to see that the greater the hurt, the greater the blessing that will come with forgiveness. Christ was God manifest in the flesh. We are to be Christ manifest in the flesh. I am in need of forgiveness from others. How can I expect forgiveness from God and others when I am not willing to give it? Are my standards greater than God's? "Blessed is the man whose sin the Lord will never count against him?" (Romans 4:8) When I forgive, I allow the Lord to bring healing into my life. "For I will restore health to you and heal you of your wounds,' says the Lord." (Jeremiah 30:17) For all that was taken from me, He has exchanged it with Himself. That's the meaning of atonement: exchange. That's a truly amazing trade-off!

CHAPTER 16

Minarets in the Middle East

"I am not the same having seen the moon shine
on the other side of the world."
~ Mary Anne Radmacher-Hershey

*Travel is fatal to prejudice, bigotry, and narrow-mindedness, and many of
our people need it sorely on these accounts. Broad, wholesome, charitable
views of men and things cannot be acquired by vegetating in one little corner
of the earth all one's lifetime." ~ Mark Twain*

TURKEY

MARCH 1999

THE FIRST TIME we were privileged to take an international trip was
to the ancient land of Cappadocia, part of modern-day Turkey. When I
first met a talented and enthusiastic lady named Cathryn soon after we
moved to Aiken in 1985, little did I know what a great friendship was

being forged. In 1990, when the Lord called Cathryn and her husband Andy to minister in Turkey, Cathryn asked me to be their vital link. A vital link is a representative from our church who keeps the line of communication vibrant between the person in the field and our sending church. Over the years, our families became very close.

Our trip to Turkey almost didn't happen. Shortly before we were scheduled to leave, a terrorist group in Turkey began committing acts of violence, including a series of car bombings targeting foreign visitors and tourist areas. What was supposed to be a fun family trip now took on the grim foreboding of potential disaster. We relied on our friends to advise us as we all anxiously watched the news and prayed. Once again, we were learning that many of God's greatest gifts come when we receive them by faith, trusting Him even when situations ahead look ominous. Two days before we left, I read the following poem and felt very much encouraged to move forward.

Afraid? Of what?
by E.H. Hamilton

To feel the spirit's glad release?
To pass from pain to perfect peace,
The strife and strain of life to cease?
Afraid? Of that?

Afraid? Of what?
Afraid to see the Savior's face,
To hear His welcome, and to trace,
The glory gleam from wounds of grace,
Afraid? Of that?

Afraid? Of what?
A flash – a crash – a pierced heart;
Brief darkness – Light – O Heaven's art!
A wound of His a counterpart!
Afraid? Of that?

Afraid? Of what?
To enter into Heaven's rest,
And yet to serve the Master blessed?
From service good to service best?
Afraid? Of that?

And so, in a step of faith, and with encouragement from Andy and Cathryn, we made our first trek across the ocean on March 26, 1999. We flew on a Swissair 747 from Atlanta, Georgia to Ankara, Turkey arriving on Saturday, March 27. It was the only international trip that all four of us have ever made. Dan and the kids had the thrill of a lifetime when they were allowed to step into the cockpit and watch the pilots in mid-flight. This is now unheard of with post-9/11 airline security requiring locked cockpits while in flight.

Andy and Cathryn were amazing hosts and tour guides, and, as always, the Lord delighted us with many unbelievable extravagances along the way. When we arrived in Ankara, we had to pinch ourselves that we were able to travel to such an exotic country for which we had prayed for so many years. Again in God's providence, we arrived the weekend beginning the Christian Holy Week.

The night we arrived in Ankara, the city was bustling with a flurry of activity equivalent to our Christmas Eve as citizens busied themselves shopping and making preparations for the following day, the Kurban Bayram, or Sacrifice Holiday. This is a major event in the Islamic calendar. It commemorates the occasion in the Quran when Abraham was prepared to sacrifice his son upon the command of God. God interrupted the act, and Abraham used a ram instead. This is a yearly sacrifice of a cow, goat, or sheep. These days, the sacrifices take place in seclusion, but in 1999 when we were there they were performed in front courtyards all over the city.

The day after we arrived was Palm Sunday, March 28, 1999. I was in the bedroom desperately trying to manage a Turkish keyboard as I typed a quick note to Grace Church of Aiken, to tell them we had arrived safely and to give a brief update. From the living room I heard 12-year-old Aaron excitedly shout, "Mom, come quick, they are slitting a goat's throat!" Not a phrase I was used to hearing coming out of my son's mouth.

He had his face pressed against the apartment living room window that faced the courtyard several stories below. We watched in horror as a Turkish family gathered around and ceremonially hung the goat upside down and slit its throat while Andy explained why this was done. The sacrifice is purely obedience to a command because sins are addressed in a very different way in Islam. Muslims are expected to give a third of the sacrifice to the poor and share a third with family and friends, and can keep the remaining third for themselves. The Red Crescent (the Turkish version of the Red Cross) encourages people to donate the skins to support their work. What a shocking immersion into the Islamic Turkish culture!

The city of Ankara is quite hilly, affording clear views of courtyards and front yards all over the city. As we drove to church that morning, we witnessed families sacrificing animals at every turn. I'm sure my jaw hung open as we drove past scene after scene of bloody sacrifice, and at one point even witnessed the total beheading of a bull. The more disturbing and moving emotion came from the knowledge that these acts were being done in futility to atone for the sins of the people. I cried with compassion for the souls of the Turks as I recalled the truth of Hebrews 10:4: "It is impossible for the blood of bulls and goats to take away sins."

When we finally arrived at The International Protestant Church of Ankara (IPCA), the scene stood in stark contrast to the morning activities we had previously witnessed. We had prayed for nine years for this church that our friends helped lead. The front wall of IPCA is floor-to-ceiling rounded glass through which one can clearly see the city. I was flooded with gratitude to God for bringing me to this amazing church in this part of the world that He had laid on my heart.

About the time I gained my composure, the music started. Once again I was overcome with emotion – this time one of overwhelming humility and gratitude for the exquisitely precious One Who paid the perfect sacrifice: the perfect, unblemished Lamb, the Lord Jesus Christ.

Truth is liberating. On this day, Palm Sunday, I was surrounded by voices lifted in praise to the Lamb of God Who takes away the sins of the world, a stark contrast to the vain and empty sacrifice of bulls and goats witnessed through the front glass of the building. My desire to see the gospel shared in this part of the world was further cemented that day as I was reminded how unworthy I am to have had my eyes opened to the truth of God that Christ died once for all. "... so Christ was offered once to bear the sins of many. To those who eagerly wait for Him He will appear a second time, apart from sin, for salvation." (Hebrews 9:28) The contrast was profound. I have tasted of the Lord, and He is good.

Our families spent the next nine days traveling all around the country from Cappadocia toward the Syrian border, hugging the Mediterranean coast and visiting many of the churches of the book of Revelation. We dipped our toes in the Mediterranean in Iskenderun, went to the Apostle Paul's home at Tarsus, and took a Mediterranean boat ride sailing from Antalya. We touched the warm pools just above Laodicea in an area called Pamukkale, the site of ancient Hierapolis. We took a rough ride over stony paths to find a few broken pillars from the ancient city of Colossae. There we shared communion on huge boulders at the site of St. Philip's martyrdom. We saw the great excavations of the mighty Biblical city of Ephesus where we sat in the magnificent amphitheater in which Paul preached and the Ephesians shouted for two hours, "Great is Artemis of the Ephesians" in Acts 19. In each city we visited, Andy read the corresponding Scripture written to or about that city. The Lord was revealing Himself to us, and it was just as dramatic and stirring as it sounds.

TURKEY

OCTOBER 1999

"Yet I will not forget you. See I have inscribed you on the palms of My hands."
Isaiah 49:15

On August 17, 1999 a 7.4 magnitude earthquake struck the area of Izmit, Turkey. It lasted less than one minute, killing approximately 17,000 people, injuring 200,000, and leaving around half a million people homeless. Even though official sources put the casualty count at 17,000 people, unofficial estimates are closer to 35,000. In October of that year, Dan and I returned to Turkey to work at a refugee camp provided for earthquake victims by World Relief, a Christ-centered, nonprofit organization which provides humanitarian aid and emergency relief in disaster areas.

At the request of Andy and Cathryn, our church responded to the earthquake by sending several teams to help with relief. Dan, a friend named Virginia, and I traveled to Turkey just a month and a half after the earthquake.

The week before we left, I received a phone call from our friend Mike who was providing emergency medical care to the earthquake victims near Izmit. He started the phone call by describing the scene before him. He was sitting in a refugee camp and was overlooking the Sea of Marmara on the Turkish shoreline. As he was treating patients, a nurse approached to ask for his help. She said she had a Turkish woman who insisted on seeing him after she heard he was from the United States.

Her name was Nurhan, and through an interpreter he learned that her home and business were destroyed in the recent quake. She and her family had escaped with nothing but the clothes on their backs. When she heard he was from the States, she excitedly asked if he could get word to her family in the U.S. to let them know she was alive and well. She had tried in vain to contact her family through the Red Cross. Because of the extensive destruction, chaos and staggering death toll caused by the massive quake, the Red Cross had been unable to help her. Her family in the States was just as unsuccessful in their efforts to find out whether she and her husband and children were dead or alive.

Mike told her he would try to get word to her family if he could contact them in the U.S. When he asked where her family lived, he was astounded when she answered, "A small town called Aiken, South Carolina." Mike knew this was the hand of God. To my further astonishment, when Mike called with the name and location of her family in Aiken, I realized that these family members were acquaintances of mine, whom I'd known years earlier in the homeschool network. We knew God was once again enjoying showing off His mighty hand. He was orchestrating a special mission for us as we prepared to travel for our own earthquake relief work in that same camp a few weeks later. I had the fabulous experience of going to their home in Aiken and being the good-news bearer to Nurhan's family in the States. We rejoiced at the chain of events that brought this family together in a time of great need.

Dan and I became friends of her family in the States and were able to take gifts and notes from them when we went to Turkey a few days later. We had a very special, providential meeting with Nurhan and her family who were living in temporary housing near the seaport city of Izmit. As we sat in their cramped kitchen sipping strong Turkish tea, we were all moved to tears as we gave them the gifts from their American family who had so lovingly chosen each one accompanied by hand-written notes of love.

For ten days Dan and I had the privilege of working in the World Relief refugee camp. We labored alongside staff and volunteers from around the world. My duties included helping to organize the gigantic tent that housed supplies such as body bags, blankets, food, and medical supplies. These supplies would be distributed to many such refugee camps around the country. People who became displaced during the earthquake, and the tremors that followed, found themselves living in cardboard boxes around the countryside trying to escape the rain and chill of the coming winter months.

Volunteers traveled from all across the globe to provide tents for temporary relief. We had the unique experience of working with men and women from Germany, Romania, South Africa, England, and Iran as well as with other Americans and Turks. One of our greatest blessings was seeing the "Body of Christ" from around the world, their expression of worship, and their talents being brought together to serve other human beings in need.

The refugee camp where Dan and Virginia and I ministered was a temporary tent city. Dan worked with the men as they created more permanent housing out of shipping containers. We watched as one delighted family after another moved into dwellings that were little more than sheds. Each one was about the size of an average-sized American living room, with no kitchen and no bathroom, but the families were truly grateful. Dan worked hard, helping pour concrete for a recreation tent for this prefab "city," digging ditches, moving concrete block foundations for the units, and setting up huge metal containers used for storage and distribution of relief items.

Our day started long before 7:30 a.m., which was when the group of volunteers gathered for breakfast and devotions. We slept in sleeping bags in unheated, ill-lit U.S. Army tents that did not quite manage to keep out the winter rains. Volunteers and earthquake victims lived side by side in the tents with plenty of opportunities for interaction, hugs, affection, words of encouragement, expressions of concern, and practicing our language skills on one another. The first few days, Virginia and I were assigned to organizing relief items like sleeping bags, blankets, food, and clothing and preparing them for shipment to distribution centers throughout the earthquake zone.

Virginia took on the role of the chief cook for the camp of over 50 volunteers after the missionary who filled that job became bedridden with the flu. Since Virginia had previously been a cook working for a boy's camp, she was the perfect candidate – really the only candidate – for the job. She and I were responsible for three large meals a day for the camp workers, who were expending so many calories doing heavy physical labor. I became her sous chef and was grateful she knew what she was doing as we toiled to provide the only source of nourishment for the entire camp. We were up before the break of dawn at zero dark thirty, just after the first Islamic call to prayer.

By the time the men were awake and ready to eat, Virginia and I had miraculously whipped up a hearty and nourishing breakfast to feed them. Since we were on a very limited budget, provided by the agency, and were stretched to the max, there were many times Virginia and I went hungry as we served everyone else ahead of ourselves. I am sure the workers thought we had extra food in the kitchen for ourselves, but I learned sacrificial giving when Virginia held nothing back but served our entire resources to these burly, hard-working men. It was grueling, physical labor of pushing wheelbarrows and carrying water buckets, running on little sleep in cold, muddy surroundings, but it was one of the most exhilarating experiences of my life.

The most exciting day for the earthquake refugees was moving day. This was a day of rejoicing when dozens of earthquake victims living in this camp moved into the prefab units. They were the first in the country to move into more permanent housing since the earthquake had taken its toll in August. Many had been living in cardboard boxes on the street and then in Army issue tents, so these prefab sheds were luxurious in comparison. There was an abundance of tears of joy and hugs as we celebrated with them as one by one they received the keys to their new homes. They were extremely grateful, and we felt honored to be there to witness the culmination of what so many teams before us had worked so hard to achieve.

Another fun serendipity of that experience was our ability to meet Benjamin, the son of pastor, author, and speaker John Piper. Benjamin was one of four young Moody Bible College students who heard about the disaster and decided to take a semester off to minister to the earthquake victims. These young men brought great fun and life to the camp and were definitely favorites of the children in the camp.

Before leaving the country, we drove along the Sea of Marmara through the earthquake zone from the coastal city of Izmit through the towns of Adapazarı, Gölcük, and Yalova. It was intensely moving to see the vast amount of devastation that mere seconds of seismic activity had caused. Building after building in town after town looked like a scene from a war zone. Winter was fast approaching, and still in every city and village families were living in tiny government-issued tents or lean-tos they had built from plastic and cardboard. Through several hours of driving, almost every empty lot or park or highway median was occupied by families now living in tents.

Two weeks before we left for this trip, the Lord spotlighted a verse for me while I attended a weekend retreat. "Where there are no oxen, the stable stays clean, but from the strength of an ox comes an abundant harvest." (Proverbs 14:4) The point was made that every decision and choice we make has at its root a desire for either ease and comfort (the clean stable) or a willingness to be in on what God is doing (the abundant harvest). If we choose to live for the abundant harvest, then dealing with the messy stable is secondary because that's just part of the harvest. For us, this recent trip to Turkey was partaking of just a small piece of God's abundant harvest. There was, however, plenty of mess in the stables in the form of a 14-hour plane flight each way, jetlag, sleeping in a cold, wet tent, seeing horrific devastation, and physically working harder than we had in a long time.

But oh, the harvest! God shows again and again that just like the acorn falling into the ground and becoming a mighty oak tree, out of death springs forth life. Even in the midst of this tragedy, the Lord was bringing about an abundant harvest for the people of Turkey. Many of our family and friends were in on that harvest by helping with donations, taking care of our children while we were out of the country, providing us rides to the airport, and just plain ol' moral support.

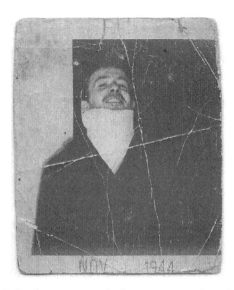

My dad, John Margo, in a body cast in November of 1944

Dad had graduated to a neck brace in this photo taken in 1945 at Fort Story,
Virginia Beach, Virginia

Peggy's first holy communion photo. It was around this time that I first felt a tug from God on my life.

Fun with Turkish antiquities, Ankara, Turkey

Virginia and Peggy with earthquake victims at the World Relief refugee camp near Istanbul, Turkey, October 1999

Being greeted with flowers by my African son, Emmanuel, in December 2012 in Bangui, Central African Republic

Dan and Peggy in Murren, Switzerland

View from the foot of Brumbach Falls, Braunwald, Switzerland

CHAPTER 17

Hinds' Feet on High Places

Though the fig tree should not blossom
And there be no fruit on the vines,
Though the yield of the olive should fail
And the fields produce no food,
Though the flock should be cut off from the fold
And there be no cattle in the stalls,
Yet I will exult in the LORD,
I will rejoice in the God of my salvation.
The Lord GOD is my strength,
And He has made my feet like hinds' [deers'] feet,
And makes me walk on my high places.
- Habakkuk 3:17-19

Western Man Study Tour
Germany, Italy, Austria, and Switzerland
2001

During her freshman year at Columbia International University, Ashley came to tell us about a study tour that was available to students. It was called The Western Man Study Tour, and Ashley desired to go. Although this was something that she really wanted, she simply gave us the information and left it up to us to say "yea or nay." The tour was designed to expose Bible College students to international missions and to give them a vision of what God was doing around the world. This particular tour was guided by CIU staff and was worth college credit. The trip included Germany, Italy, Austria, and Switzerland. As Dan and I discussed the benefits of this study, Dan suggested that we not only help fund Ashley, but that I also go along since they were in need of a few adult chaperones. Ashley and I were beyond thrilled!

This was truly the trip of a lifetime. We spent 10 days traveling to cities like Florence, Italy, Venice, and Salzburg, with an emphasis on church history and world evangelism. Along with our CIU tour guides, there was a handful of adults and close to 30 students. It was invigorating being around so many young people who were experiencing this part of the world for the first time. Although I thoroughly enjoyed the entire trip and learned many things about church history, culture, foods, and architecture, for me the two countries where God showed Himself personally to me were in Italy and Switzerland.

While on tour in Florence, Italy and about to see the incredible statue of David sculpted by Michelangelo, a professor on our tour read Psalm 147:10-11 which says "He [God] takes no pleasure in the strength of a horse or in the legs of a man. No, the LORD's delight is in those who fear Him, who put their hope in His unfailing love." Michelangelo's David is a masterpiece of Renaissance sculpture. It is a stunning example of a statue bearing an amazing likeness to the human body. The legs of David are impressively human, down to the anatomical intricacies of muscles, veins, and arteries. However, the professor was reminding us that although this statue impressed us, nothing – absolutely nothing – delights the heart of God like those who put their hope in Him. Do I want to delight the heart of God? The only way to do that is to put my entire trust in His unfailing love and by faith trust His promises. God thirsts to be thirsted for. God was wooing me to rest in Him. I will forever be reminded of that truth whenever I see a photo of Michelangelo's David.

The spiritual pinnacle of the trip for me, though, was the time we spent in Switzerland. As I mentioned earlier, one of the biggest tools the Lord used in bringing me to a deeper walk and greater knowledge of Him was the book, *Hinds' Feet on High Places.* I devoured this book while going through cancer treatment and the very painful physical and spiritual challenges of 1994 and '95. The scenes of nature, and corresponding spiritual truths, that are described in the book gave me a deep sense of awe for the Swiss Alps. Although it never crossed my mind that I might ever visit Switzerland, like most little girls my age I grew up with *Heidi* and *The Sound of Music*, with their larger-than-life portrayals of the majesty and culture of the Swiss and Austrian Alps.

As a young girl, another of my favorite movies was *Almost Angels*, an obscure movie about the Vienna Boys Choir filmed in Austria. In my chaotic and less-than-glamorous life growing up in a very rough part of town in the coal community of Wilkes-Barre, Pennsylvania, Austria and Switzerland seemed to me to epitomize serenity, beauty, and tranquility. Though I never even dreamed of traveling there, in my mind, to live in Switzerland meant to live close to heaven.

Hinds' Feet on High Places is an allegory that dramatizes the journey each of us must take before we can live in the "high places" of love, joy and victory with God. The book is based on Habakkuk 3:19 and Psalm 18:33: "The Lord God makes my feet like hinds' [deers'] feet, and sets me upon my high places." It was written by Hannah Hurnard in the remote Swiss village of Braunwald. Hurnard wrote the book while on a three-week visit to Switzerland on her way back to her ministry as a missionary in Israel. She had just returned from a short visit to England following the death of her father. During those three weeks, the Lord gave her the premise of the book based on her experiences in this tiny village, which is nestled in some of the most spectacular vistas of the Swiss Alps.

When our study tour group arrived in Switzerland by bus, I could hardly contain myself. I would like to say that being in Switzerland was a dream come true, but the truth is, it was beyond my wildest dreams!

And as if that wasn't enough, in following years I would be blessed to visit Switzerland an unbelievable five times thanks to Aaron's parental flight benefits, including three visits to Braunwald itself.

Our first day in Switzerland found us arriving in Interlaken, which means "between the lakes," in the Bernese Oberland between Lake Thun and Lake Brienz. What opened up before us was one of the most spectacular scenes God has ever created. As we drove, we came through the Lauterbrunnen Valley, known as The Valley of 72 Waterfalls. Before me, I saw beauty unspeakable. The 72 waterfalls gush down into the valley from the vertical cliff faces towering hundreds of feet above the valley. The magnificent landscape makes a lasting impression. The lush and glorious valley is surrounded by immense cliffs over which come these roaring waterfalls. Lifting my eyes, I looked across the valley at the towering snow covered peaks above.

The whole neighborhood is filled with the sound of rushing water pouring down over and between the rocks. I recalled the words I'd read in the book,

> "I have been brought to a place where all God's creation appears to be uttering things in a language which only becomes clearly audible and understood by hearts that have been learning in the school of suffering. It is the language which one begins to spell out in one's innermost soul when one is on the cross to which self is being transfixed by nails of pain and anguish of heart."

Referring to the waterfalls pouring themselves down in an extra-ordinary ecstasy of self-abandoned giving, Hannah Hurnard writes,

"Watching the waters as they leap over the edge, and following them with my eyes as they fall downward, I discover that the whole movement is one of the most breathtaking examples of utter rejoicing and of triumphant, almost delirious abandonment that I have ever seen. If one looks at the falls as a whole, they are marvelously beautiful. But if one gazes at one particular part of the water as it plunges over the lip, and then watches it as it falls right down, the almost crazy, blissful abandonment is staggering. I never saw motion so utterly expressive of joy. The movement looks like perfect rapture, fearless surrender to a hitherto un-known delight, the greatest it is possible to experi-ence."

The message of the waterfalls is one of humility, "the pouring of oneself down lower and lower in self-effacement and self-denial. The message of running water always is "Go lower. Find the lowest place. That is the only way to true fulfillment." The poured out life gives life and power to others. The more love gives, the more it fulfills itself." Summed up in the words of an old Quaker lady, "Self-sacrifice is the ecstasy of giving the best we have to the One we love the most."

Up to that point, I had shared a hotel room with at least one other person in the group. I longed to be alone with the Lord while in Switzerland. When we arrived at our castle converted into a hotel, to my delight the tour leader asked if I "wouldn't mind" staying in a room alone while we were in Switzerland. Mind? I was thrilled to pieces and saw this as another gift from the Lord. I distinctly remember overflowing with gratitude and awe for the Lord as I entered my private sanctuary. Could God really love me so much that He brought me to the Swiss Alps to spend several days communing with Him in the majestic Swiss countryside which I had so longed to see? The thought was staggering. Through my open window I heard the only things audible in this quiet valley: the sound of falling water and the bells of the cows as they graze on the mountain slopes. I fell to my knees beside the bed and wept, utterly overwhelmed by His goodness to me. "Oh my Lord! How undeserving I am. But how I thank you!"

The next morning several of the braver souls in our group headed for the mountain tops. The highest slopes are connected by a combination of funicular trains, cable cars, and Sesselbahn (chair lifts) slung across the rocky slopes. I longed to ride in one of these cable cars since reading about them as Hannah Hurnard experienced them some 50 years earlier made a great impression on me. I was anxious to boldly display the trust I had in God's ability to hold me from above. About 20 of us boarded a series of cable cars leading to Schilthorn, a mountain peak nearly 10,000 feet in elevation. As the first cable car lurched away from the building with a great swoosh, several of the college girls let out a nervous giggle and clung to me for stability. I was at the front of the glass cable car, in ecstasy and exhilarated to experience this symbolic trip as an outward sign of my inner surrender to God's future plans and purposes. The whole thing had now become a symbol of my abandonment and reliance on God. The ascent of the cable car and the spectacular views it afforded of the gigantic mountains surrounding us and the quiet valley below was as close as one could be to flying like a bird. As we were lifted upward, I echoed the author's thoughts described as she watched these cable cars and chair lifts:

> "The cable by whose power they traveled overhead was quite invisible. Underneath there was nothing but the abyss, and no earthly ground of support. But they were supported from above. The power came from above, and by means of that power they were able to travel upward, in defiance of the law of gravity. They went higher and higher, fixed with the wheel which ran up one cable and down another. One had only to be willing to trust the invisible power and abandon oneself completely. No self-effort was possible. Then one would be wafted up toward the heights. It was all a matter of faith and no works except for the initial work of choosing to abandon oneself to the Sesselbahn.
>
> How like that overhead cable the promises of God often seem to be. They look so appallingly frail and unsafe and without earthly support of any kind, apparently leading to such impossible situations. It

seems they certainly cannot be relied upon, for we tell ourselves how easily we may be mistaken and claim what was never meant for us personally, but only for the great courageous saints of God, prophets, and apostles.

But once we abandon ourselves to these promises, and enter into them in the abandonment of faith and obedience, then all the overhead power begins to work. The traveler resting on and in the promise does nothing but remain in it. Having trusted the promise enough to risk everything upon it, up one goes! And no power on earth can hinder arrival at the consummation of the promise and its perfect fulfillment. Though we may seem to meet the most horrifying precipices confronting us, and abysses far below which we could never hope to ascend nor pass over in our own strength, yet in the spiritual Sesselbahn of faith and obedience, everything is triumphantly surmounted."

"God is not a man, that He should lie... Hath He said, and shall He not do it?
Or has He spoken, and shall He not make it good?"
- Numbers 23:19

On June 7, 2013 Dan and I returned to Braunwald, Switzerland. I had recently been diagnosed with back problems consisting of severe degenerative disc disease, spondylolisthesis, and severe spinal stenosis. For almost six months prior to the trip I had intense pain in my back and down my legs and hip, as well as numbness and tingling in both legs, which caused me to limp for several months. Even after nearly three months of physical therapy, I was experiencing unrelenting pain and limited mobility performing my day-to-day tasks.

The discomfort was more severe when climbing stairs or walking on an incline. If I could barely manage to get around the house. How did I ever expect to hike in the Swiss Alps? I was taking a prescription-strength painkiller, which in itself was causing my normally low blood pressure to climb to dangerous levels. I had tingling over most of my body, now accompanied by hot flashes and red cheeks which, though I later learned they were a side effect of the pain medicine, were frightening at the time. So it was with much fear and trepidation that we approached our departing date. We almost cancelled several times.

The morning of our flight arrived, and I awoke with just as many symptoms as ever. I felt weak and anxious with the unknown symptoms, which I was beginning to think indicated a much more serious, systemic problem. The thought of traveling in such physical distress made my knees shake. I did what I've learned to do so many times when faced with a terrifying situation: I fell to my knees and prayed. I told the Lord that even though it seemed risky to take a trip like this right now in view of my back and hip pain and multiple unexplained symptoms, I knew He was my Creator, and I knew I could trust Him to lead me wherever He wants me to go. As soon as I finished, I got up from my knees to fix my makeup and hair while I listened to the audio version of *Hinds' Feet on High Places* that I had downloaded on my phone. It started where I had left off the day before, chapter 7:

> "'My sheep hear my voice and they follow Me. This is the path you are now to follow. Remember, Much-Afraid, whenever you are willing to obey Me and to follow the path of My choice, you will always be able to hear and recognize my voice. And when you hear it, you must always obey. Remember also that it is always safe to obey My voice even if it seems to call you to paths which seem impossible or even crazy.' On saying this, He blessed her."

I stood stunned as once again God answered my cry in such a pointed and specific way. Those words gave me the courage to board our plane and trust my future to Him. To my amazement, the more we climbed the Braunwald Alp, the more my tightened muscles and tendons improved. The remainder of my alarming symptoms disappeared when I discontinued the pain medicine. Each day I improved more and more, and Dan and I were shocked at the stamina and strength I exhibited on our daily hikes, which often lasted eight hours or more a day. That was the beginning of my understanding that although my degenerative disc disease is never going away, staying active with moderate exercise and stretches is key to living with these issues.

It was another step in realizing that I need to find God in the present and not wait for my circumstances to improve. God wants me to find Him sufficient in the midst of trouble rather than just demanding that He deliver me from it. As Vivian Greene put it, "Life is not about waiting for the storm to pass, it is about learning to dance in the rain." Once again, I trusted God when all the odds were against Him, and He victoriously brought me through. "Let the beloved of the LORD rest secure in Him, for He shields him all day long, and the one the LORD loves rests between His shoulders." (Deuteronomy 33:12)

CHAPTER 18

The Least of These

in the Heart of Africa

"Our goal is to comfort the afflicted and to afflict the comfortable."
~ Wes Stafford, Compassion International
Child Sponsorship Ministry

"The eye never forgets what the heart has seen."
~ African Proverb

CENTRAL AFRICAN REPUBLIC

JUNE 2006

IT IS DIFFICULT to go back to a normal, ordinary day once you have tasted purpose. I've learned so much from the brave men and women of the Central African Republic (CAR). In this impoverished country, I learned that I may not be able to change the world, but if I let God use me, I might be able to make a small impact in somebody's world. Many things in my life have caused me to initially draw back in dread and then have challenged me to walk by faith with God. The majority of those were situations in which I had absolutely no control, and I would have rescued myself out of them in an instant if it were within my power to do so. To me it's one thing to hold God's hand as I enter an inescapable hardship, but quite another to actively volunteer for a situation that scares me to death.

All three of the times I've been to the CAR would fall into the latter category. I suppose my caution is understandable when you consider the risks and demands of visiting one of the poorest, most dangerous countries in the world. Consequently, it amazes and delights me that time and time again I find myself compelled to do things that frighten me simply because I know it's what God wants me to do. Yes, going to CAR the first time was a very scary thing for me. But God put it on my heart, and I have learned that when He requires something of me, it's up to Him to enable me to do it. Peace lies on the other side of obedience. I love Francis Chan's description of this kind of faith-stretching situation.

> "The greatest blessing I received in the inner city was seeing God work in situations where He has to. As a result, I've made it a commitment to consistently put myself in situations that scare me and require God to come through. When I survey my life, I realize that those times have been the most meaningful and

satisfying of my life. They were times when I truly
experienced life and God." (Francis Chan, *Crazy Love*)

My love affair with the people of Central African Republic started in earnest in 1989 when some of our dearest and most incredible friends, Mike and Myra, moved there as medical missionaries. The Fellowship of Grace Brethren Churches has a history of over 90 years of missions in the CAR, and our church in particular became totally invested when Mike and Myra were sent out from Grace Brethren Church of Aiken. As confidantes of our God-saturated friends, we spent many hours praying with them and for them when they first felt the call to go.

In 1989 we threw them a big party and bid them farewell. That initial year saw many letters going back and forth from Bangui, CAR to Aiken since snail mail, hand-carried by another missionary, was the only form of communication back then. It was a big deal to place a phone call to them on the very rare occasions when we knew they were in a city where they could be reached, perhaps at the home of the American ambassador. Even then, the connections were poor, the time delay required one to say "over" at the end of a sentence, and there was a great monetary cost for even a few brief minutes. When Mike and Myra first went, I had a heart for them and their calling. By the end of that year, God placed on my heart a love for the people of CAR and His work in that country that went beyond my relationship with my missionary friends.

In 2003, war broke out in CAR. The effects of that war, coupled with the AIDS crisis, left CAR even more impoverished than before, and now with an extraordinary number of orphans. Almost every home in CAR had many orphaned children living in it, as the people of CAR care for their orphaned relatives. It was not uncommon to speak with adults who were responsible for 17 or more children. The burden was immense and these precious African families were at the breaking point. These were the poorest of the poor.

Around that time, three Central African women began inviting orphans to their homes to provide schooling, meals, and Christian education. Grace Brethren International Missions (GBIM) partnered with these women to create Project Hope and Charite (PHC), a team that loved Jesus and thought of serving orphans and widows in the CAR as a way of serving Him. The PHC team consisted of the board of directors and teachers comprising Central Africans as well as a volunteer staff in the United States. Almost 2,000 orphans were paired with American sponsors who provided monthly for their needs.

Thanks to improvements in technology that made intercontinental communication easier, sponsors were able to have one-on-one relationships with their children, and two-way correspondence by mail became a major part of what PHC staff provided. The kids came to PHC during the day to receive Christian schooling and meals, but they returned home to their extended families in the evening. Encompass World Partners, the cross-cultural ministries arm of GBIM, also invests in Hand-in-Hand Orphan schools, small church-based schools in many villages of CAR that are paired with sponsoring churches in the U.S.

I had already become intimately aware of and invested in the work and ministry in CAR for over ten years as Mike and Myra lived and worked there. I was hooked financially, prayerfully, and emotionally. Therefore, it wasn't surprising that my heart felt a tug when in 2006 several ladies in our church had the opportunity to go there on a short-term mission trip. At that time GBIM sponsored short-term missions trips made up of laypeople working in areas where the church already had a presence. These teams were called GO (Global Opportunity) Teams. The group from our local church consisted of Deborah, Laura, Rebekah, and myself. This particular GO Team was requesting women who were willing to work with orphans and widows through the ministry of Project Hope and Charite.

The prospect of finally being able to travel to this country I had grown to love was both thrilling and frightening to me. This was another example of God motivating me to do something for others which they could not do for themselves simply because God had done for me what I could not do for myself. We were each required to pay our own way, almost $3,000 per person. I also had my doubts that I would be cleared medically since I have chronic lymphedema in my left arm, which leaves me vulnerable to life-threatening infections. Even if I were able to afford this trip, could I do it physically? I had my doubts, but to quote Pastor Steve, "Faith believes that God will give me the grace to handle the things I'm dealing with."

Since my initial struggle with phobias and fear, I've found many times that there are only two choices when I am faced with something that I'm convinced God wants for me but which frightens me: to move forward by faith, or to turn back and risk becoming a prisoner of the fears that stunt my potential in God. It seems as though these smaller fears pale in comparison to my ultimate fear of missing out on God's best for me. This excerpt from *Hearing Heart* by Hannah Hurnard propelled me forward:

> "You too are afraid of some giant in the way before you. Never fear. Meet him in the name and strength of the God of David, and though you feel like a grasshopper in comparison, he will fall to the ground before you. God's love shut me up to two alternatives: I must either follow Him no matter what He asked me to do or turn back to the old nightmare existence of being imprisoned in myself."

I voiced my initial concerns about health issues and finances to Deborah, the lead member of our team at Grace Church. Deborah had been a missionary in CAR for several years herself. When I told her I had a great desire to go but I wasn't sure it would be possible, she said, "Just the fact that you have a desire to go is an indication that the Lord is prompting you." Then she questioned, "Do you have any idea how few women have the desire to go to CAR?" I never gave it a thought that my desire to minister in CAR wasn't something every woman craved. She also reminded me of Philippians 2:13: "For it is God Who works in you, both to will and to work for His good pleasure." Deborah quoted the old adage, "Where God guides, God provides." I was learning to trust the truth when God calls you to do something extraordinary, He empowers you to do it. Sure enough, every door opened, including a positive response from Dan and others, medical clearance, and help from unexpected sources with funding.

What followed were months of preparation including multiple team meetings, various mandatory vaccines, language study, required reading, and much prayer. One of the most daunting tasks on any trip is packing. Each of us was able to take up to 100 lbs., but what to pack was further complicated by the fact that we were trying to take very few personal items in order to leave room for supplies to be given to the Africans themselves. With their needs being so vast, how could I justify taking frivolous personal items like a hair dryer and curling iron? We were about to minister in one of the poorest countries in the world, a country in which the average income is less than $2.00 a day, where the average citizen has no electricity, inadequate health care and, at best, questionable drinking water. No, most personal items would be left at home.

The best way to describe all of my experiences in CAR was one of "controlled chaos." Scrap wood is used for heating and cooking on outdoor fires. The resulting smoke is combined with the acrid odor of gozo, the staple food of most Central Africans. Gozo is a sticky paste made out of the manioc or cassava plant. It has little nutritional value but does have the benefit of making one feel full. A cloud of smoke hangs over the city, and the smell of burning wood, coupled with the sour smell of cooking manioc, produces a stench that permeates every building, every piece of clothing and every nostril in the city. I learned on subsequent trips that as soon as our plane landed and the doors were opened, I could tell we were in Bangui because of that undeniable smell.

Opportunities abound to try exotic foods in CAR. I ate many different foods, including the gozo I mentioned earlier as well as "mystery meat" cooked in questionable sanitary conditions prepared by the widows. We were told not to ask what we were eating, and I didn't. Perhaps the most exotic critter I ate while in Africa was a big, fat, juicy termite. Termites grow quite large in the CAR. Going to the open air food market in Bangui was quite a shock to the senses. I saw, smelled, and touched things I'd never seen before such as fried caterpillars and the aforementioned termites, which I'm told are a good source of protein. So, like any self-respecting short-term missionaries, we bought a bag of termites, and took them back to the mission station for the African ladies to prepare. Termites were just one of the many side dishes we had for dinner that night. I must admit I enjoyed the cooked termite more than I ever imagined I would. It was crunchy and tasted a lot like a bacon bit.

Alexandrine was the African Director of PHC. Alexandrine was also a midwife who directed many other midwives. Soon after we arrived in CAR we met with Claudia, Suzanne, and Alexandrine, the three ladies heading up the African side of PHC. One of their original members had since passed away at a young age. Our team leader and U.S. Director, Barb, was there when that brave soul was dying, and Barb had promised to do everything in her power to care for her children who would be left behind. This calling had become personal for Barb.

At our first meeting, Alexandrine shared with us how in her midwife practice when poverty-stricken women came to her clinic desiring an abortion, it was her custom to remind them, "God has a plan for your child." She would urge them to at least deliver the baby and pray about adoption. She found that the vast majority of women were willing to deliver their child with the intention of later placing them for adoption. Once the mother delivered her baby, it was cleaned up, clothed, and lovingly placed in the mother's arms. Alexandrine wisely let mother and child spend lots of time bonding. After a while when she would ask them to hand the baby over to be given away, the vast majority of mothers adamantly refused to let their babies go. As a matter of fact, out of the thousands of babies that were delivered under her care up to that point, only three mothers chose adoption and two of those three infants were adopted by Christian parents.

Each day our team would go to Alexandrine's front yard, where we held Bible-school-type activities with the kids. The first day we arrived, we expected to teach around 15 orphans but were shocked when more than 50 kids arrived. The absolute joy of these kids and their enthusiasm and great gratitude to be included was unbelievable. I was so impressed to see older kids helping the younger ones. When one received a letter from their American sponsor, the whole group celebrated. They seemed to be genuinely thrilled for one another. This was in stark contrast to the selfishness and jealousy that all too often defines kids in the U.S.

One day the plan was for the children to make beaded bracelets. They were to produce one for themselves and one to be mailed to their sponsor. This was to bond sponsor and child together. The bracelets were comprised of plastic string like fishing line strung with tiny multicolored beads. The task was much more difficult and time consuming than we originally expected. Here were these poor kids painstakingly putting one bead on at a time only to have several fall off. It took forever to string enough for one bracelet let alone two. If the string was mishandled while finishing it by tying it, off slipped all the beads that had taken upwards of an hour to string.

Working in the hot sun, it became apparent that completing the bracelets by tying the fishing line required too much manual dexterity for the majority of the kids. That became the job of the adult helpers. One by one, each of the kids proudly held up their finished product for us to complete. I had gotten overheated and couldn't seem to cool off. The scene is still vivid in my memory as I recall the intense sun glaring down, roosters crowing in the distance, mosquitoes landing on me, limited communication skills, dusk approaching, and a mixture of sweat and bug spray making my hands as slippery as ice.

Looking back, it was such a trivial thing, but my worst fear was that I would drop each bracelet and destroy the tireless efforts of these tiny cherubs. I remembered God's promise in Philippians 2:13, and I prayed, "You called me here to do this, Lord, please enable me to do what you brought me here for." With that, my energy level lifted, and I didn't drop one bracelet. Time and time again, when faced with similar situations, I relied on the Lord and found that He gave me more than enough energy to do what He called me to do.

During my first week in CAR, as we instructed the orphans I noticed a hardworking, older-looking boy who appeared to be around 14 years old. Most births are not documented, so it's not uncommon for these kids not to know their exact birth date or age. Part of our preparation for this trip was being informed of cultural "do's and don'ts." While we would think nothing of inquiring of a child in the U.S. what their age is, it is understood that this is not a question one asks in CAR. When I questioned the African leaders about this boy, I was told his name was Emmanuel. He was the son of a deceased pastor. Emmanuel had begun hanging around PHC but was told that he was too old for the sponsorship program. Undaunted, Emmanuel continued to volunteer his time by helping the younger children. He was a kind and tireless worker who was as reliable as the noonday sun.

Emmanuel had been laboring for weeks, getting absolutely nothing in return. I learned he was also a leader among his peers at church. As I watched Emmanuel throughout the week, I was impressed by his humble, servant spirit. He was pleasant, friendly, and had a great sense of humor even in very trying circumstances. Between my extremely limited Sango (the native tribal language) and pantomime, Emmanuel and I became fast friends who worked well together.

I had come to CAR asking God to show me which orphan He wanted me to sponsor. We were to leave the country in just two days, and most of the kids we were teaching already had sponsors. Back at the mission station Barb and I were sitting at the computer looking through photos and matching kids with their names and their sponsors' names looking for kids who needed a sponsor. Emmanuel was in the back row of one of these photos.

"Can I sponsor him?" I asked.

She shot back, "Him? I don't even know his name."

"It's Emmanuel M____, and he's a great kid! I was told he was too old for the program. Can I sponsor him?" I had my fingers crossed.

"Of course!" came her response. It was a match made in heaven.

That afternoon I went to the tiny Christian bookstore on the mission station and bought Emmanuel a Sango Bible. I wrote him a note explaining that God had placed him on my heart for him to become my son. Barb translated the note into Sango. The next day, the last day we would see the kids, hardworking and loyal Emmanuel was there as usual laboring away and getting nothing in return.

Barb called him over and explained that I had been praying for a child I could sponsor. As she put her arm around him and talked to him, I could see Emmanuel look over the sea of kids in front of us, wondering which of the kids I had chosen. She told him, "God chose you, Emmanuel!" His eyes got big and he and I choked back tears as the reality of it dawned on him. We embraced, and I gave him the Bible I had bought for him along with the letter and picture of my entire family. We spoke for several minutes as Barb translated for us and he called me Mama Peggy. It was soon time for us to leave, but it was with a happy heart that I waved goodbye to him and promised to return as he had asked. I'm thrilled to say that I was able to return to see him in 2008 and in 2012 as our relationship has deepened over these many years.

In 2008, on my second trip to Bangui, I traveled with Lois to visit her daughter, Laura, who was working full-time with the orphans. Laura was also helping a young couple who were leading an abstinence based club called True Love Waits. It was inspiring to see Laura and this young couple challenge teens to wait until marriage to become sexually active, a notion as rare in this part of Africa as it is in the United States.

One of the highlights of that trip was an opportunity to accompany Emmanuel to his home. On the way to his home, Emmanuel took us through tall bush and dirty river water. I was aghast to find out that the filthy, muddy river water where people bathed and animals drank was the same water Emmanuel and his family used for drinking. I was able to visit his mud hut home, meet several of his family members, and help fund him to learn how to sew. The heart-wrenching truth that I could not rescue Emmanuel and his family out of that situation really hit home with him a few days later. Emmanuel had the mistaken notion that his sponsor, Mama Peggy, would whisk in and fly him out of there back to the United States with her. I'll never forget the day that I explained to him (through my translator) that the laws in his country as well as mine would make it absolutely impossible for that to happen.

The moment the following day when we embraced and said goodbye on a busy street corner, with tears streaking our faces, is firmly and painfully etched into my memory forever. It's during times like these that I struggle to trust God without understanding His purposes. In *A Step Farther* Joni Eareckson Tada says,

> "What a mistake to think that I would ever be able to complete the whole puzzle of suffering. For wisdom is more than just seeing our problems through God's eyes, it is also trusting Him even when the pieces don't seem to fit."

Emmanuel will always be my son. I'm broken-hearted to say that as of this writing the ravages of war have once again come to this country, creating upheaval and turmoil. Conditions in CAR are worse than ever before in recent history. Fighting has brought chaos, death, and famine to the land. But my devotion to Emmanuel has not waned. We estimate that Emmanuel is now most likely in his early twenties. It has become more difficult than ever to communicate, due to a nonexistent postal system and evacuation of our missionary friends made necessary by the extremely dangerous atmosphere there.

The last time I saw Emmanuel was in December of 2012, just five days before murderous rebels overtook his homeland. Looking back, it is clear that our team got out of the country just before all hell broke loose. Although I had no way of knowing the coming events, the day we said our goodbyes I was compelled to pray with Emmanuel and to remind him repeatedly that even if he didn't hear from me, he could rest assured that he was not forgotten and that he was forever in our prayers. Myra, Emmanuel, Judith (my daughter's teenage orphan daughter), and

I stood in a tight circle with our heads touching and arms tightly over each other's shoulders as we prayed with them and reassured them of our commitment to them and love for them.

Recently a fellow worker and friend of mine, Brenda, put herself in peril to go to CAR to work with the Hand-in-Hand schools. At great personal risk, Emmanuel was able to come to the mission station to meet with Brenda and receive the funds and letter I sent. She found out that he is married and has a one-year-old son. I was pleased to know that he is strong and healthy. This young man who grew up without a father is now a father himself.

"When a brave person takes a stand, the spines of others are stiffened."
- The Summit

These words define many of the persons I have come to love in CAR. I suppose one of the reasons I keep being drawn to return is the fact that my own spine has been stiffened by those whom I now have the privilege of calling my friends. I've learned from these saints that resilient people will not betray their values when they struggle. On the contrary, they find purpose in their suffering. I'm inspired by remarkable men like Pastor Andre, the Grace Brethren pastor who risks his life often to minister in very treacherous parts of his country. He has a passion for the spread of the gospel that is unparalleled. Pastor Andre is an amazing man of God who has endeared himself to anyone who knows him and has become like a brother to our pastor.

I've had the honor of getting to know Francois and his wife Claire. Francois is the Director of the Seminary in Bangui and has been a target of the rebels in recent months. He relayed the story of a group of rebels entering his church and kidnapping him to hold him hostage for money. As the rebels were leading Francois away, his congregation bravely came outside and surrounded them. The rebels decided if they couldn't capture Francois, they would kill him. They fired several shots at Francois at point blank range before they were chased off by the crowd. Expecting their pastor to be dead, the group was amazed to see Francois get up from the ground, unscathed by the bullets. They were unable even to find where the bullets had landed. Napoleon Bonaparte himself recognized that "Jesus alone founded His empire upon love, and to this very day millions would die for Him." Francois is one who is willing to risk death in order to share the love of Christ with others.

Augustin is another mighty man of God. God is not looking for extraordinary people. God is looking for ordinary people who will trust an extraordinary God, and Augustin is one of those men. This man has been called to the very formidable task of promoting Christian ethics in an otherwise extremely corrupt government. God has given him audience with some of the most powerful men in the country as well as boldness to speak on behalf of Christ. Augustin repeatedly risks his life in order to minister to thousands in his country. One of those he meets with weekly is the current President of the Central African Republic. People like Augustin are living examples of a quote I heard from Pastor

John Piper: "Lives of faith are the great mirror of the dependability of God."

Dibona is another hero of the faith. Our friend, Mike, helped train Dr. Dibona. In the face of much adversity and under extremely trying situations, Dibona continues to provide medical care to his fellow countrymen, often at great personal risk. I grew to love Dibona on my first trip to CAR. As the physician who helped care for the orphans, Dibona worked tirelessly to treat the boys and girls for myriad issues that would have otherwise gone untreated. One day we met Fiacra, a little boy dying of AIDS. This little boy had the spirit of a champion, and we all fell under his spell. At his own expense, Dibona devotedly took Fiacra, the one minuscule chance of successful treatment that was available for him.

The last day I saw Fiacra, he was on the back of Dibona's motorcycle smiling and waving as they rode away. A few weeks later, Fiacra succumbed to his disease. Dibona and his wife, Denise, are currently a very integral part of Three Strands, the ministry led by my friends, Mike and Myra. Three Strands is a ministry aimed at providing compassionate, competent and Christ-centered medical care focusing on both the physical and spiritual needs of the neediest people in the developing world. These folks are living examples of the truth spoken by Corrie ten Boom when she noted, "If God sends us on strong paths, we are provided with strong shoes."

Eating in the home of Africans often causes foreign visitors to experience digestive upset in the following days, and I was no exception. After being up all night with an upset GI system, I felt like a whipped puppy the next morning. Laura, her mom, and I had been invited to travel to our Bible College in M'Baiki, a village several hours' drive to the south. I wanted badly to go but feared the ride along the bumpy dirt roads where bathroom facilities are nonexistent. Once again, I prayed and took the leap of faith, deciding the worst thing that would happen was that I would be trampled by an elephant while squatting in the bushes in the middle of Africa – a fascinating story for my descendants to tell of how grandma died.

I knew I had made the right decision when I boarded the vehicle and Tim, our driver and long-time missionary, congratulated me for taking the risk of coming when I wasn't feeling well. He confirmed that pushing ahead and trusting God was the bold thing to do as he saw many who shrunk back and let fear stop them. I was overjoyed when I felt better as the day wore on, and our time at the Bible College was filled with marvelous times of laughter, encouragement, and fellowship with the seminary students and their families. It was my first time squatting over a hole in the ground to go to the bathroom, but at least it was in the village and not along the road on the way.

The language barrier is a frustrating hindrance when you are a gregarious person who loves to "go deep" with people right away. I've been told by those in the know that foreigners are very appreciative when an American attempts to speak their national language. I think it's pretty well known around the world that most Americans are not bilingual. Therefore, before traveling to another country I try to learn a few key phrases in the national language. I was at least able to greet the Africans in their natural tongue and make an attempt at niceties such as asking, "How are you?" and answering, "I am fine." As we said farewell to the director of the Bible College, I spoke some of my limited Sango and said, "Nzapa abata mo," which loosely translated means, "May God be with you." Pastor Egbeya stopped in his tracks and with a look of great pleasure declared to those around him, "Oh, listen to those beautiful words coming out of her mouth!" He loved hearing his mother tongue from me. Don't we feel the same way? How much more does it thrill the Lord to hear us speak well of His Son!

Full-time aid workers and missionaries address enormous spiritual, medical, and physical needs. Our team's impact would be a drop in the bucket compared to the need, but we answered the call and, I'm sure, received more than we gave. We had the great privilege of spending a good amount of time with a large group of widows, women who have experienced the ravages of war and the loss of their husbands and, along with that, any financial means of support. Thankfully, there are missionaries with much more talent and ability than I will ever have who are attempting to meet the vast medical and financial needs of these women by helping them start microenterprises and gardens.

But how do you emotionally support someone who has been so deeply wounded? How do you make a difference in someone's life in a few short weeks when their needs are so vast and so completely beyond your abilities? Won't anything you do be "too little too late"? I didn't have a clue, but here is what I learned: you pray, and you listen to men and women who have listened to the Lord and who know His answer to those questions. I found that the answer to those questions is the same the world over. It's the same whether you are ministering to widows and orphans of war or to a lonely neighbor across the street. You simply love them. You love them with the love of God that is beyond your own ability to love, the love that He supplies. You open yourself up to them and share your own vulnerabilities. You love them without a word just by truly listening to them, by looking them in the eye and showing them that you care, that they have immense value in God's eyes and are worth traveling halfway across the world or across the street for. You hold them with arms that are safe. You cry with them. And, maybe even more importantly, you laugh with them as together you learn that "He will once again fill your mouth with laughter and your lips with shouts of joy." (Job 8:21)

I've gotten to know and have grown to love many of these coura-geous women. One of my favorite memories is the day Barb arranged for us to pamper a group of these widows who work tirelessly and who never stop serving others. She lined up others to care for their children for a few hours, a rarity in their lives. Barb and several of us baked chocolate chip cookies and took them with us. With the ladies seated in a large circle, we waited on them hand and foot. We served them our homemade cookies and lemonade. After their snack, our team knelt down in front of each one and, one by one, lovingly washed their feet before presenting each one with new shoes and placing them on their feet. We cried together. We giggled together. We clung to each other with more demonstrative affection than I think I've ever experienced in one place in my life. When the women of the Central African Republic are especially joyful, they break out in spontaneous, lively singing. This day, there was much singing. It was a blessed day, and I am certain that I gained more courage and encouragement from those special women than I could have ever hoped to give. Finally, Barb encouraged the women with teachings from Scripture from the book of Ruth, who was herself a widow. "May the Lord God of Israel, under whose wings you have come to take refuge, bless you for it." (Ruth 2:12)

My heart continues to be drawn to these captivating people as I am inspired by the faith and resilient spirit of the Christians I have met there. They have so much less than we have, but they do so much more with the little they have. I have never witnessed such a joyful spirit as I have among the African Christians. They are extraordinary people. The Scripture spoken of the Israelites enduring slavery in Egypt seems to apply to my suffering friends: "The more they afflicted them, the more they multiplied and grew." (Exodus 1:12)

CHAPTER 19

Parenting 101

"Our children are messages we send to a time we will never see."
~ Neil Postman

"Has not the Lord made them one? In flesh and spirit
they are His. And why one? Because He was seeking godly
offspring. So guard yourself in your spirit."
~ Malachi 2:15

I HAVE OFTEN stated that being a parent is one of the most challenging yet rewarding things I have ever done. The most difficult thing about being a parent is that the minute you become pregnant, you begin to realize that, although a separate human life is being entrusted to you, that life is almost completely outside of your control. Becoming a parent is one sure way to recognize that most of the circumstances in our lives are out of our control. Our homes are merely incubators for the lives that have been entrusted to us. Incubators were never intended to last forever. Some of my greatest spiritual growth has come from the adventures of being a parent. The disciples saw Jesus turn water into wine and they said, "OK, life doesn't have to be normal." Whenever we are blessed to watch God work, we walk away changed forever.

When I became pregnant with Ashley in 1982, I had a very strong desire to be the kind of parent God wanted me to be. Sadly, I have come up short in that goal many times. But, early on, what enticed me to be obedient to God was the marvelous blessing of seeing God work in my life and the lives of my children.

The first time God reminded me that my unborn baby was His and only on loan to me was soon after we found out I was pregnant. I started to have abdominal pains and feared that I was going to miscarry. I was utterly amazed at how maternal I felt toward this life that was within me, and the thought of losing that life terrified me. I had to pray and tell God that, although I passionately desired to deliver a healthy baby, I trusted Him and His wisdom. Another time was when I was nearing my due date. One night I had some frightening medical symptoms. Dan was working out of state, and I was afraid I was going into premature labor and would have to deliver alone since my extended family also lived far away.

We were planning an unmedicated delivery and had attended Lamaze classes together. Home alone that night, I called Dan on the phone, crying and telling him about my concerns. While I talked, our cat, Nikki, jumped up on the bed next to me. She started panting and looking distressed. I kept talking to Dan and more or less ignored her because of my own distress. In a matter of minutes, our kitty gave a gentle push and out popped a beautiful little kitten. I hadn't even known she was pregnant. I was astonished! Witnessing the speed and ease of that delivery was like splashing a cup of cold water on my irrational fears. It was as if God was saying, "Childbirth is the most natural thing in the world. If I can do this with a helpless little cat, how much more can I carry you through?" God had spoken loud and clear, and I was His humble student. I spent the remainder of the evening delighting in the new little kitten and praising the Lord for calming my fears.

Sure enough, Ashley was delivered in an unmedicated birth in Wilmington, Delaware on December 27, 1982, nine days before her due date. The birth was almost as quick and easy as the one I witnessed with our cat. I was delirious with joy at being a new mother. While we were in the hospital, Ashley had a lot of phlegm in her lungs and throat and had to be aspirated by the nurses occasionally. When this happened, Ashley would appear to be choking, throwing her arms straight out in distress and turning dark pink. It scared me to death, and although we had rooming in and kept Ashley right next to us, I was grateful that there was a nurse's station and nursery adjacent to each room. The nurses showed me how I had to suction the phlegm from Ashley's mouth and throat to clear her airway. I held onto that little blue suction bulb like a lifeline.

We were discharged from the hospital the day after her birth, and I couldn't wait to bring Ashley home. Dan lovingly got me settled into bed with Ashley sleeping in her bassinet next to me while he returned to work for a few hours. It was a glorious, sunny day as I lay there feeling like the most blessed woman in the world. All was well with the world. I rolled over and dreamily began to drift off into sleep. Oh no! I sat bolt upright. The thought occurred to me, "What if the baby begins to choke while I'm asleep? She could die. I can't fall asleep. I have to stay awake and make sure she's OK. I have to keep her alive. As a matter of fact, I can't fall asleep tonight either. I can never fall asleep!"

The absurdity of that last thought dawned on me. I recognized that it was God who held Ashley's breath in His hands, not me. "In His hand is the life of every living thing, and the breath of all mankind" Job 12:10. He was the giver and sustainer of life, not me. He had her days numbered, and it was not up to me whether she lived or died. Again, He was asking me to trust Him. I acknowledged my foolishness before Him and asked Him to forgive me. Ashley was only two days old, and this was at least the third time I was being reminded by God to hold on to her loosely. It's a lesson I've had to learn with my children time and time again. And if truth be told, I'm still learning it.

My second born, Aaron, was such an easy child. As a baby, he smiled all the time at everyone. People didn't even have to be looking at Aaron. If another person walked into the room, Aaron made eye contact and smiled his infectious smile. I am so happy to say that Aaron is still that way today. Aaron's entertaining sense of humor has been a great source of refreshment in our family. Throughout Aaron's life, I recall so many times when things would get stressful. To the surface would rise

Aaron's subtle humor and the tension was dispelled immediately. What a gift. I'm sure that trait, along with Aaron's generous spirit, have been two of the many reasons why he has never lacked for friends.

Having learned to release my first child to God helped me to hold on a little more loosely to my second. Although I'm sure there were many times when he was younger that I had to release Aaron to the Lord, one of the most striking times was the day he got his driver's license. Aaron was Mr. Popularity. Everybody wanted to be his friend. Not only that, but during his high school years it was quite common for parents to approach me to tell me that they wanted their son to be friends with Aaron because he was such a good influence on their boys. Mothers were always trying to fix Aaron up, not just with their daughters but also with their sons for his good influence.

Since Aaron was always accompanied by a herd of guys, I knew that as soon as this young man got his driver's license, I would rarely see him again. Before he had his license, he and his friends hung out at our house all the time. I knew wheels would change all that. Add to that my exaggerated fear of motor vehicles. My mother lost a four-year-old child born before me to a truck accident. I grew up hearing details of this tragic accident and saw the ongoing anguish in my mother's heart. I witnessed firsthand how the devastation of losing a child never ends. My kids learning to drive was my worst nightmare. Pine Log Road was a busy, four lane road that bordered our neighborhood. Since there was no traffic light at the entrance to our neighborhood, getting in and out of the development was challenging, especially during the evening rush hour.

The day finally arrived for Aaron to take his driver's test. He passed on the first try. Just my luck! We got home from the DMV at rush hour. Sure enough, as soon as we got home Aaron asked the dreaded question: "Can I have the car to go tell my friends?" I couldn't come up with a good excuse to say "no." Handing him the keys felt like the umbilical cord was being cut all over again. As Aaron excitedly dashed out of the house, I went to the bedroom and fell to my knees next to my bed. Crying, I asked God for the grace to release Him and symbolically let him go. I was terrified that Aaron was going to get creamed before he even left our neighborhood. Imagining him trying to enter traffic scared me to death. I was so lost in my thoughts that I didn't hear Dan come home from work and walk in the house. He entered the bedroom, and I looked up, surprised to see him. As I dried my tears, I told him the news.

"Aaron passed his driver's test and he just left to tell his friends," I sniffed.

"I know," said Dan casually.

"How could you know?" I asked.

"I saw him driving out of the neighborhood. I was the one who stopped in traffic to let him out."

I was shocked! What were the odds that on his first attempt to the leave the neighborhood the boy's father would be the one who would give him the right of way to pull out into traffic? The timing had to be perfect for that to happen. I saw it as a direct answer to my prayer. God was reminding me once again that He was in control and the divine

Orchestrator of all things. I was in a battle with God for sovereignty. I was learning that when self is first, peace is last. If God is sovereign over my life, then certainly He is sovereign over my kids' lives too. The people God uses the most are the ones who hang onto the least. Although it might be a frightening thought, that also includes letting go of our children.

Letting our children grow up and have lives of their own is difficult for any parent, including me. All four of my kids, including my kids-in-law, have grown up to be pretty amazing people. They are the kinds of people that attract others to themselves. They are impassioned, adventurous, fun-loving, generous, lighthearted, hard-working servants. All four of them are conscientious, thoughtful, and devoted parents. They live their lives with deliberate intention, which disarms and pleases me to no end. I honestly couldn't have chosen anyone better to parent my grandchildren. Their little ones call me Nina, and I consider it a great privilege to be grandmother to their children. Who wouldn't want to be around such folks? I feel very blessed to be a special part of these very precious lives that were only on loan to me from the start.

In the year or two after I wrestled with breast cancer, Ashley was just 11 years old and Aaron was 8. We were your typical busy American family involved in public school, soccer, basketball, and so on. I was the average mom worrying about my kids' grades, health, athletic prowess, and future careers. As I pondered my priorities in raising my kids and knowing my time could be short, I came upon these verses:

"Let not the wise boast of their wisdom
or the strong boast of their strength
or the rich boast of their riches,
but let the one who boasts boast about this:
that they have the understanding to know me,
that I am the LORD, who exercises kindness,
justice and righteousness on earth,
for in these I delight, declares the LORD."
(Jeremiah 9:23-24)

What that said to me was that although the American dream is to have kids who have wisdom, strength, and riches, the thing that would impact the lives of my kids and set the tone for their fulfillment was the knowledge of the God Who created them. Nothing else would ever come close to that. A paraphrase of that verse I heard is, "Trust not in your brains, body, or bucks, but in the Living God." Although we continued to be involved in sports and the usual all-American pursuits, I began to put more energy into teaching my kids about their Audience of One, the only One Who would ever truly satisfy them. My kids are far from perfect, but I can say that they seem to have found the real meaning to life, and they know the source of their joy is Christ.

I watched as many families in our church homeschooled their kids. As a matter of fact, at that time the vast majority of the kids in our church were homeschooled. I craved what I witnessed in these families: kids who were doing well physically, emotionally, and most of all, spiritually. I also knew there are absolutely no guarantees in childrearing no matter what route one takes. Jesus was perfect, and His disciples were still disobedient to Him at times. God was the perfect parent to Adam and Eve who rejected His will and sinned. Still, I became convinced that homeschooling my kids was the best chance I had of giving them a healthy spiritual future. After all, your thoughts are where your choices are formed. I wanted to promote right thinking in my children.

Aaron was excited about the prospect of homeschooling. Since most of his closest friends were already homeschooled, he didn't worry about losing out socially. If anything, I think he knew that less time in the classroom meant more time socializing. Ashley, however, had her reservations. I tried not to force the issue but spent a lot of time in prayer. If God truly was the one calling us to this, then He had to be the one to bring the kids and Dan, who was also reluctant, on board. It was a matter of the will and not of emotion to honor God with faith when the future was uncertain.

One of Ashley's greatest concerns about leaving public school was that it meant giving up her potential involvement in a program called Kennedy on Stage. This was a very popular song and dance program sponsored by Kennedy Middle School, the school she attended. Ashley had a good voice and was quite coordinated. She had every reason to believe that she would participate in Kennedy On Stage the following year. As a matter of fact, a teacher and the club's director told Ashley to make sure she tried out for it because she was a shoo-in to make it.

My journal entry for May 2, 1996 says, "Ashley prayed that if she didn't make Kennedy on Stage, that would be a sign to homeschool. She didn't make it." She reluctantly agreed to be schooled at home.

Although it was a struggle for Ashley, the Lord showed up in many ways to confirm our decision. On August 19, 1996 we started our first day of homeschooling. Ashley was in 8th grade and Aaron in 5th. I knew the first day of public school would be difficult for Ashley. Providentially due to my sister's schedule, the first day of public school that year "happened" to be the day that our family left town on our way to Hilton Head for vacation with my sister and her family. I remember Ashley's delight as we drove past her old school and she waved toward the school and said, "So long suckers, I'm heading to the beach!" The humorous thing is that as I write this in 2014, Ashley is homeschooling her firstborn. I'm sure the Lord loves to bring things full circle like that.

Although I considered homeschooling my kids to be a tremendous honor, and I had the support of my friend, Beth, and many other friends, there were times when I was scared to death. The task of teaching my kids was daunting. I was making the choice to teach my children at home for their spiritual benefit, not because I had any measure of confidence in my own ability to teach. I came upon the following writing around this time, which undergirded my determination to accept the challenge:

FORTITUDE

"Fortitude is moral courage, the strength to persevere

and do the right thing in the face of adversity or challenge. We have no guarantee that doing the right thing will make us comfortable, successful, or even happy. In fact, doing the 'right' thing is often costly to our immediate happiness. Ask the martyrs of old if standing up courageously is easy. Ask Wilberforce, who stood up against the slave trade. Ask Thomas Moore, who stood up for his own conscience against the command of his king. Ask Dietrich Bonhoeffer, a brilliant theologian and pastor who died at the hands of the Nazis.

Fortitude is the ability to hang in there even when doing the right thing extracts a price. It is the ability to courageously obey the dictates of our conscience rather than follow expediency or comfort. Life presents us with many temptations; fortitude is the ability to keep on doing the right thing no matter what the immediate consequences." (*Children of a Greater God*, Terry Glaspey)

CHAPTER 20

Aiken Christian School

"Therefore, I have lent him to the Lord.
As long as he lives, he is lent to the Lord."
~ 1 Samuel 1:28

ONE OF THE best words of advice on schooling my kids came from my former pastor's wife, Pat. As I was grappling early on with decisions about private vs. public school, she reminded me that I could decide on their schooling one year at a time and not feel like I couldn't make changes the following year. That thought occurred to me just a year later when several men and women in the community were led to start a new Christian school in Aiken called Aiken Christian School (ACS).

Knowing the passion of these leaders and learning about the mission of ACS convinced us it would be a good place for Ashley. Although she was embracing being schooled at home and was especially thrilled with the homeschooling co-op that we joined, I knew she craved a formal classroom setting. Ashley was an excellent student who missed participation in a class and the positive feedback she got from others.

Although the school board of ACS had other students they intended to interview before Ashley, the evening they started their interview process "coincidentally" found all these students preoccupied with other events. Ashley became the first student they scheduled to interview. The board was unanimous in accepting Ashley as a student and felt like she epitomized what they were looking for: someone who excelled in academics as well as character and integrity. When we walked out of the doors of the school with Ashley being congratulated as the first official student of Aiken Christian School, I saw it as further confirmation that we were making the right decision. Around that time, my father decided he didn't want to wait until he died to give his children the little bit of money he saved as an "inheritance." His desire was to disperse it to the four of us that year and enjoy watching us spend it. Although it amounted to a relatively small amount of money, it was almost exactly what we needed to pay Ashley's tuition for the year in full before school started which allowed us an additional discount.

The following year, we decided to enroll Aaron at ACS as well. Being able to afford private school for both of our kids was a huge concern. Staying home to raise my kids was a top priority for me. I transcribed medical records for an oral surgeon just a few hours a week and worked during times when Dan was able to be home with the kids. I told the Lord I was willing to work more hours if He chose to use my earning potential as the answer to our financial concerns. Within two weeks of that prayer, I was offered three jobs totally unsolicited. The day after I prayed that prayer, I came to work at the oral surgeon's office. The receptionist told me that the previous day a young patient had asked the staff if they knew of a medical transcriptionist who was looking to work more hours. The patient was an employee at a cardiology office, and they needed a part-time transcriptionist. They gave her my name. This busy cardiology practice was more than willing to let me work during the hours my kids attended school and stop work in time to pick them up from school. By May 9th of the following year, we had the total tuition for both kids in our savings account. Once again, God was giving us confirmations on this road. I was learning that God's work, done in God's way, will never lack God's blessing.

CHAPTER 21

Moms in Touch

"If you find a path with no obstacles, it probably doesn't lead anywhere."
~ Frank A. Clark

IN 1997 WHEN Aiken Christian School was being formed, I heard that they were choosing teachers and curriculum. The thought occurred to me that there was a great need to pray for the school board in making these vital decisions. I sent an email to Dave, a friend and school board member, expressing my concern and suggesting that the school call parents together to pray. He sent back an unexpected note that said, "Thank you for your concern and for being willing to start the ministry of Moms in Touch at ACS." I was flabbergasted! Was that what I said? I didn't think so. As I thought about his comment, however, I realized that if God was putting it on my heart that a prayer group be formed, perhaps He was asking me to form it. It didn't appear that anyone else had the same burden. Pastor Charles Stanley is quick to say, "Be obedient to God and leave the consequences of your obedience to Him."

Although I had never led a prayer group before and the idea frightened me, I was motivated by the bigger fear of being disobedient if I didn't forge ahead to be the founder of Moms in Touch at ACS.

What followed were many years of God revealing Himself to me in mighty ways as I led Moms in Touch at Aiken Christian School. God was asking us moms to pull up a front row seat and watch Him work. The satisfaction of knowing God and doing His will was more of an attraction than the emptiness of the world. Moms in Touch, which is an international organization now called Moms in Prayer, is made up of mothers of students who get together weekly to pray for their children, school, and teachers. Week after week, our hearts cried out to God on behalf of our children. It nourished my soul to be with other women of great faith.

We followed the suggested model to pray the ACTS prayers - to begin with Adoration, move on to Confession of our sin, then Thanksgiving followed by Supplication or sharing our petitions. Many had a regular habit of praying that if the students were doing something wrong, God would expose them. Although we gathered for the benefit of our children and the school, we grew spiritually ourselves. Prayer is a means of growing in an intimate relationship with the God of the universe. Instead of problem-centered prayers, we were learning God-centered praying. We were finding satisfaction in Him so the lure of the world wasn't quite so strong. Watching the Lord work in the lives of these students was thrilling as we learned that the dreams of one generation often become the realities of another. Answers to prayer were a consistent source of joy for all of us.

CHAPTER 22

Columbia International University

*"I have no greater joy than to hear
that my children are walking in the Truth."*
~ 3 John 1:4

I FIRST HEARD about Columbia International University (CIU) in 1994 when I began reading books about and by Robert C. McQuilken, the first president of CIU. As I read some of McQuilken's writings, I was incredulous that there was a college that taught the victorious Christian life and that, unbelievably, that college was just an hour away in Columbia, SC. My children were in elementary school at the time, but I hid that information in my heart. Years later when Ashley was due to graduate from Aiken Christian School, I encouraged her to consider attending CIU. She was not interested. Although I thought CIU would be a great choice for her, once again it appeared that God was leading me in a way that my husband and children didn't embrace. How illogical did it appear to have Ashley attend CIU when she could live at home and attend a secular college at much less expense? Besides, CIU didn't even offer a nursing program, which at the time was her area of interest. However, Ashley attended a college fair where a representative from CIU asked her to come for an overnight campus visit. Surprisingly, she agreed. A week later she visited the campus.

I'll never forget the look on Ashley's face when I arrived at the school to pick her up. I spotted her in a sea of students, and her face was radiant. She had had a wonderful experience and said that the words of the school president, Dr. Murray, made a powerful impact on her when he said, "If you don't know what God wants you to do with the rest of your life, what better place to find out than at a Christian college?" She agreed to attend for their one year Bible certificate program while she prayed about her future.

In God's sovereignty, she would attend CIU for a total of six years, receiving both her bachelor's and master's degrees there, finishing early, and graduating with honors. She even worked there for a short time after graduation. No doubt her years at CIU equipped her perfectly for the important calling God had for her life of ministering side by side with her future husband, Jim, as the influential spouse of an Army Chaplain. A year after Ashley started at CIU, Jim also enrolled and eventually completed his bachelor's degree as well as his Master of Divinity.

Although Aaron was always Mr. Compliant and up to that point had never given us any discipline problems, his first year of college was a rocky one. During that freshman year at the University of South Carolina's Aiken Campus, Aaron seemed to be drifting away from us and further from God. In the early spring of 2005, Dan and I had a serious talk with Aaron about his future. The three of us agreed to pray together that God would show us where He wanted Aaron to go to school the following year: USCA, CIU, or Charleston Southern. As Aaron flatly, reluctantly prayed with us while seated at our kitchen table, I made note of the fact that he was sitting in the exact same seat that Ashley had sat in ten years earlier when she reluctantly prayed about homeschooling. Witnessing the astounding things God was doing in and through Ashley gave me great faith as I saw what fantastic things God could do with a reluctant prayer.

I spent many hours trying to convince Dan to fund Aaron's education at CIU, but Dan was hesitant to pay college tuition for a son who was not fully convinced that he should attend that college. Between Dan's reluctance to pay the tuition and Aaron's lack of desire to go, it seemed a long shot that this would ever happen. Once again I had to put my emotional blinders on and walk by faith with my eyes on God as I felt sure I was following His urging. The day I took Aaron's application for financial aid, I walked all around the campus praying specific, intentional prayers for Aaron at each site. During that brief time when Aaron seemed cool toward the things of God, I was told I could pray a verse for my child 24/7 (24 hours a day, 7 days a week). Specifically,

Jeremiah 24:7: "I will give them a heart to know me, that I am the LORD. They will be my people, and I will be their God, for they will return to me with all their heart."

I fasted and prayed that prayer many times for my son. In August 2005, Aaron began attending CIU. By the end of Welcome Week, the Lord had a hold of Aaron's heart. On May 9, 2006, Aaron was asked to give a devotional message to seniors at the Grace Brethren Church Junior-Senior Banquet at Newberry Hall, a confirmation that Aaron's spiritual growth was evident to many others as well.

CHAPTER 23

Our Family Grows

"But as for me and my household, we will serve the Lord."
- Joshua 24:15

AARON EARNED A bachelor's degree at CIU, but he found an even greater treasure there. CIU is where he met Katherine, his future wife. Katherine is the perfect mate for Aaron. As we got to know her, we realized what an honorable woman she was. Kat impressed us with her intelligence and strong work ethic. She was good with money, self-disciplined, beautiful, and a real go-getter, someone we thought would make a great wife and mother. After they dated for a while and we knew Aaron was contemplating making Katherine his life partner, Dan had a talk with him. "Katherine is a very sharp young lady. You don't want to let this one get away," he counseled him. With the blessing of all four parents, Aaron had the good sense to propose to Katherine soon after that.

Jim and Ashley first met during their 9th grade of Aiken Christian

School. That year while Dan attended one of ACS's basketball practices, a very unusual thing happened. It was early in their initial year at the school, and Dan didn't know Jim at all. After walking through the crowd at this particular practice, Dan sat down next to me in the stands but looked a little bewildered and shaken. He asked me the name of one of the blonde-haired young man out on the court. "Jim Murray," I answered. "Why?" He wouldn't tell me what had happened, just that I needed to remember this moment for future reference. I thought the remark was strange, but I soon forgot all about it.

It wasn't until years later that Dan told me about that fateful day. As Dan walked through the players on the basketball court during their practice that day, God strongly impressed upon him that the young man who just ran past him on the court was to be Ashley's future husband. It wasn't until the night of Jim and Ashley's engagement almost seven years later that Dan shared his experience with Jim and Ashley. What a confirmation!

I've known Jim now for almost 18 years, and I can't imagine loving him more if I had given birth to him. Jim is one of my biggest cheerleaders, and he has proven to be one of my greatest sources of inspiration with his appetite for adventure, his servant spirit, and zeal for the Lord. Jim Murray can never be accused of staying in the still calm of life. He is a stallion, wild at heart with an adventurous spirit. Jim had a desire to serve the Lord that impressed us while he was still in high school. He also knew from an early age that he wanted to be married and to be a father.

Martin Luther describes the attributes of a good marriage when he declares, "Let the wife make her husband glad to come home and let him make her sorry to see him leave." I am thrilled to say that Jim and Ashley, as well as Aaron and Kat, seem to have that type of a marriage. When I look at my children and the mates the Lord has chosen for them, I think of the words in 1 Thessalonians 3:7-8 "So we have been greatly encouraged in the midst of our troubles and suffering, dear brothers and sisters, because you have remained strong in your faith. It gives us new life to know that you are standing firm in the Lord." I am so overjoyed by God's goodness to me that I can attest to the fact that I have found 3 John 1:4 to be true: "I have no greater joy than to hear that my children are walking in the truth." My children are walking in truth. It honestly doesn't get any better than that!

As a parent, the greatest thing I will ever raise my children to do is to obey God, even if it hurts me. Following God's leading has led to all four of my children moving away from Aiken. But perhaps the greatest test of my faith with regards to my children has been the call Jim and Ashley have felt to serve God with a career in the Army Chaplaincy. Abigail Adams was the wife of John Adams, the first Vice President and second President of the United States, and she was the mother of John Quincy Adams, our sixth President. Incredibly, she wrote this challenge to her son when he was less than ten years of age. God used this note by this great lady to remind me what He had in mind for Jim and Ashley:

"It is not in the still calm of life that great characters are formed. The habits of a vigorous mind are formed in contending with difficulties. Great necessities call out great virtues. When a mind is raised and animated by scenes that engage the heart, then those qualities which would otherwise lay dormant waken to life and form the character of the hero and the statesman." (Abigail Adams)

When God called Jim to his multiple tours of duty ministering to soldiers in Afghanistan, I once again had to rely on God's grace in order to stand behind his decision to go. It was then that the Lord brought to mind the verses in Mark 10:29 & 30, "So Jesus answered and said, "Assuredly, I say to you, there is no one who has left house or brothers or sisters or father or mother or *wife* or *children* or lands, for My sake and the gospel's, who shall not receive a hundredfold now in this time – houses and brothers and sisters and mothers and children and lands, with persecutions – and in the age to come, eternal life." I needed confirmation, and as I read this verse I couldn't deny that God sometimes calls a man to leave his wife and children to do God's will.

This quote from martyred missionary Jim Elliot's journal was another source of comfort. At age 22, Jim Elliot had a promising ministry in front of him in the United States. He could have been a very successful pastor or evangelist or teacher. His parents were not very excited about his call to go to the remote and dangerous area of the

Quichua people group in South America. They wrote and told him so.
He answered bluntly:

> "I do not wonder that you were saddened at the word
> of my going to South America," he replied on August 8.
> "This is nothing else than what the Lord Jesus warned
> us of when He told the disciples that they must become
> so infatuated with the kingdom and following Him
> that all other allegiances must become as though they
> were not. And He never excluded the family tie. In fact,
> those loves that we regard as closest, He told us must
> become as hate in comparison with our desires to
> uphold His cause. Grieve not, then, if your sons seem to
> desert you, but rejoice, rather, seeing the will of God
> done gladly. Remember how the Psalmist described
> children? He said that they were as a heritage from the
> Lord, and that every man should be happy who had his
> quiver full of them. And what is a quiver full of but
> arrows? And what are arrows for but to shoot? So, with
> the strong arms of prayer, draw the bowstring back and
> let the arrows fly – all of them, straight at the enemy's
> hosts."

> *"Give of thy sons to bear the message glorious*
> *Give of thy wealth to speed them on their way,*
> *Pour out thy soul for them in prayer victorious,*

And all thou spendest Jesus will repay."

(*Shadow of the Almighty: The Life and Testament of Jim Elliot*, Elisabeth Elliot; hymn quote from "Oh, Zion Haste")

CHAPTER 24

Puppy Dog Tales

"The dog is the most faithful of animals and would be much esteemed were it not so common. Our Lord God has made His greatest gifts the commonest."
~ Martin Luther.

"Once you have had a wonderful dog, a life without one is a life diminished."
~ Dean Koontz

OUR FOUR LEGGED FAMILY

IT SEEMS TO me that having a pet may fall into the category of God-saturated joy. If Jesus says," consider the birds," I say, "consider my dog." He loves people more than food. He overflows with affection without testing your character first. He is indomitably happy, rain or shine. He holds no grudges whatsoever, and his youth seems to be renewed like the eagle's. So if you, Father, so taught a beast with no soul, no moral or spiritual capacities to live that kind of life, how much more should his master feel ashamed that even with the Holy Spirit, I struggle to do those things.

AJAX

He was a tiny, black puff of fur with just a small shock of white on his chest. This long-haired mutt was the cutest dog I ever saw, and the first one that was mine. He was just six weeks old when we brought him home from the friend who gave him to us. Actually, the day we brought him home is one of my earliest memories. It was 1959, and I was six years old. As this black powderpuff waddled around the kitchen floor, my mother and brother prepared a box where he would sleep. The box was lined with a blanket and a "door" cut out of the side for him to get in and out. Marked clearly on the side were the large letters, Ajax. Ajax was a powdered household cleaner popular in those days. The irony here is that Ajax is a pure white powder, known for its bleaching ability. Our new puppy, black as coal, was just the opposite. Ajax. It fit. Our black smudge of a dog had his new name.

Ajax was by far the toughest dog I've ever owned. First of all, he was the only male dog I owned. But more than that, Ajax was "a dog's dog." He never had a vaccination, rarely went to the vet, didn't have a license, didn't do tricks, and roamed the city. He was like Tramp from the movie *Lady and the Tramp*, only our "Tramp" chose to call our house home.

Ajax was known by nearly everyone in the neighborhood. At an early age, he began accompanying our mailman on his daily delivery route.

Since we lived in the city, our mailman walked from house to house. Our trusty dog put in a full day's work on the daily beat and returned at the end of each day's adventure. When my brother-in-law, Jerry, became our mailman, Ajax took him under his wing and showed him the ropes. Adding to the dog's celebrity was the fact that my mother loved to drive her little blue Ford all over the city with Ajax hanging out the front window. Ajax was a rather large dog, approximately 50 lbs, and he could stand with his hind feet on the back seat and his front paws draped over the driver's side window, his head and ears flapping in the wind. I don't think Mom or Ajax were ever happier than when they were behind the wheel together. They epitomized the term, "going for a joy ride."

Ajax was a loyal dog, great with kids and mankind in general, tough as nails, but affectionate and dependable. Each day I walked home from school, as I came into view, Ajax would run across the street to greet me, which always caused me some angst since that street was Market Street, the busy, traffic-filled street on which we lived. Ajax was as faithful as they come. One day when my mom drove to the A&P grocery store, she left Ajax outside to wait for her. Typically, he was one of those dutiful dogs who would lie in front of the store without a leash. As a matter of fact, I can't recall ever seeing Ajax on a leash. He was born free and lived free. On this day, when my mom came out of the store, Ajax was nowhere to be found. Again, this was not unusual since Ajax roamed the city freely, and she knew he could take care of himself and find his way home. Mom left the store and headed home. Many hours later and long after dark we became concerned when our roaming mongrel still wasn't home. As we discussed what could have happened, we were incredulous to think he could still be at the store since it was way past the store's closing time. We hopped in the car and drove to the store, which was miles from our house. Sure enough, there was our unwavering Ajax, lying in front of the door of the darkened building waiting for mom to exit. How pitiful, yet noble. That night Ajax was rewarded with plenty of hugs, praises, and tasty table scraps.

Ajax took a lickin' and kept on tickin'. He lived to the ripe old age of 14 despite getting hit by a car in his early years. When Ajax was about 13 years old, he had advanced arthritis and began to have difficulty walking. I was a married woman and lived three hours from home by now, but Ajax was still my dog. He was like a brother to me. As a matter of fact, there were definitely times I liked Ajax better than my brother. The dog never exasperated and tormented me like John did. As Ajax's arthritis got worse and he became immobile, it became clear we would have to have him "put down." I accompanied my mom to the vet's office to have it done. She and I cried all the way there, with me sitting in the back seat with Ajax's head on my lap as I stroked him for the last time. When it was our turn, I carried him in and laid him on the cold, steel table. I was too emotionally distraught to stay and watch, so I said my goodbyes and told my mom I would wait in the car. A few minutes later as I sat in the car sniffling and drying my tears, I looked up to see my tiny mother struggling to come down the front steps with Ajax in her arms. He was alive! She explained that the vet felt that clearly we were not ready to let him go, so he offered to give him a steroid injection to see if that helped his mobility. Sure enough, within a few days Ajax was back on his route with the mailman, prancing around like he did in his glory days. We were elated! From what we were told, he even fathered a litter of puppies during that time. (Oops, did I mention he was never neutered?) But, the time finally came, a year later, when Ajax took his last ride to the vet.

POOKER

Several years after Ajax passed away, I bought my first dog as a married woman. We had been married for two years, and every young couple needs a pet to practice for parenthood. Ajax had a nickname: Pooker. Pookie, a lion puppet, was one of the characters on a popular kids' show called The Soupy Sales Show. We started referring to Ajax as Pookie, which later turned to Pooker. Sometimes we called him Ajax, but more often than not, Pooker it was. When it was time to buy my own dog, it only seemed natural to look for a black, large breed dog with a shock of white fur on her chest. That puppy we bought from a pet store in 1976 became Pooker. I used to say Pooker was part lab and part kangaroo since she jumped up so much. Pooker lived 12 years and died in 1986 just a few months before Aaron was born. One evening we called her to come in after she had been outside for a long time. She didn't come, and when we drove down Pine Log Road near our house, we found her dead along the side of the road. We took her to the ASPCA to be cremated.

Somehow we managed to remain dogless for several years following Pooker. Although Ashley and Aaron routinely begged for a dog, we opted for what we thought were less burdensome pets. What followed was a menagerie of small animals. We had four guinea pigs, Piglet being the most famous. BJ was another. Four in all. Fin Fin was a favorite fish followed by newts, aquatic frogs, hamsters, hermit crabs and a rabbit named Thumper. Ashley made a pet out of anything: tree frogs, caterpillars, and even a clam she bought at the store with daddy. I'll never forget her rushing up to the front door holding the clam in a clear plastic bag and saying excitedly, "Mommy! I got a cwam!" As strange as it may sound, the pet clam (Clammie) actually turned out to be quite entertaining for a few days as we sat it in salt water and it squirted water out of its dish by opening and closing its shell.

PEANUT

Peanut was the bodacious beagle we had while the kids were growing up. She loved to be petted, but unfortunately as she aged she became unpredictable with little kids. Peanut was a slave to her strongest sense: her sense of smell. She found every morsel of food that was dropped on the floor and when she was out on walks, once she got the scent of an animal, she looked like her nose was glued to the ground as she followed the scent with her tail straight overhead and wagging furiously. One day, while we were driving home from visiting family in

Pennsylvania, we got the call that Peanut had been taken to the vet by our neighbor who was watching her. She died that day at age 12 of bladder cancer. She lived a full life, went for long walks, ate, and appeared to be pain-free until the day she died. Not a bad way to go.

HOLLY

I must say that our golden retriever, Holly, has by far been my all-time favorite dog. I always admired golden retrievers, and after Ashley and her husband, Jim, got their golden, Carolina, we knew for sure that for us goldens rule and all other dogs drool. Even picking her out was a God thing. I knew goldens could be quite large, and I wanted a dog I could manage physically. I also wanted one who was good with children, since I was hoping that grandchildren were in our future. We wanted a yellowish dog rather than one with reddish fur. And we wanted one with a squared off face rather than pointy. We asked God to give us just the right dog.

After researching breeders and making many phone calls for just the right dog at a good price, we settled on a breeder in Appling, Georgia. When the mother delivered on Ashley's birthday, December 27th, it seemed to be another fun coincidence. We had lots of opinions in picking out a name. Dan finally suggested that since she was born at Christmas time, we should name her Holly. I loved it. She was our Christmas Holly. Dan and I went to check out the facilities and to see the pups when they were just a few weeks old, much too young to pick one out. It was decided we would choose one at four weeks and bring her home at six weeks.

The day we returned to pick out our Holly was a memorable and fun family day. We all piled into the car: Dan and I, Aaron and Katherine, and Ashley and Jim. When we got to the breeder's, he had already separated out all the female pups knowing that's what we wanted. As we walked up a slight incline, we saw a small knee-high fence where the girl pups were corralled. It was a cold winter day so all the puppies were huddled together sleeping. As we approached, I said out loud, "We just need to find out which one is Holly." As soon as I said that, our Holly walked away from the pack and came over to the edge of the fence vigorously wagging her tail. It was as if she knew her name. She was the friendliest dog by far. The entire time we held her to check her out, her little tail wagged constantly. To this day, she is still the happiest dog I know. Although she was one of the bigger dogs in the pack, I knew this was our dog. And sure enough, Holly has turned out to be one of the smallest and most manageable golden retrievers I've ever seen.

Holly took well to house breaking. Training her to come, sit, and stay was easy since Holly wants to please her master. As a matter of fact, I sometimes think it's God's sense of humor that led me to Holly. I see so many analogies between Holly with me as her master and myself with God as my Master. Like Holly, my greatest desire is to please my Master. But, unfortunately, like Holly, I have a fearful nature that leads me to tremble even when there is no danger. I see myself in her when Holly cowers during thunderstorms and hides under the bed. How many times have I run for the hills seeking cover when there was nothing to fear? "But there they are, overwhelmed with dread, where there was nothing to dread. God scattered the bones of those who attacked you." (Psalm 53:5) Good words for me and Holly.

Another time that I resemble my pup all too much is on our walks. Although she is obedient and doesn't even require a leash, Holly walks a few feet out in front of me but constantly looks back over her shoulder to her fair leader. I often think she will injure herself the way she is continually craning her neck to make sure I'm still right behind her. How much simpler it would seem for her to let me walk out in front to lead the way or at least to walk alongside one another. How many times do I get out in front of God, struggling and craning my neck to make sure He is with me when instead He longs to lead me to victory?

Something Holly dearly loves is very small stuffed animals. She is rarely without one. From the time she was a pup, we have provided Holly with an assortment of little stuffed animals, which she carries with her all day long. But the time when Holly especially searches for these toys is when she is greeting Dan or a visitor or me. Before she can greet us, Holly looks frantically around searching for a favorite toy to hold in her mouth while she wags her tail furiously and circles in a figure eight pattern around her designated loved one. I've never owned a dog that seemed so anxious to show her love and thanks to us all throughout the day, greeting us with a toy when she is in a particularly good mood even if the glorious reunion comes after a separation of just a few minutes. Every time we feed her a meal, we are rewarded with the sight of Holly with a fluff of fur held gently in her mouth and five minutes of tail-wagging joy. Could Holly survive without these adorable little toys scattered throughout the house? Absolutely. But Dan and I delight in providing them for Holly because of our love for her, much as God delights in giving me not just what is necessary for my survival, but good things simply for my pleasure. "Whatever is good and perfect comes down to us from God our Father, who created all the lights in the heavens." (James 1:17)

CHAPTER 25

Lessons Learned from a Stray Cat

ALTHOUGH WE HAVE owned several cats over the years, I often think back to the lessons I learned from a stray cat we found on the road one day. When Aaron was around 13 years old, he, Dan, and I took our dog Peanut for a walk around the adjoining neighborhood, Mallard Lake. Since it was a very quiet neighborhood, we often walked on the street. As we came around a corner, I saw a cat sitting in the middle of the road directly ahead of us. Strangely, the cat didn't run away as our dog approached. As we got closer, I discovered why: the straggly cat was emaciated and had difficulty walking. As we got closer, it began ever so slowly to stagger sideways. My first thought was that it might have distemper, or even rabies, so I warned Aaron not to let our dog get close. Although I felt pity for the cat as it staggered to the side of the road, my concern was for my son and our dog.

Suddenly, Aaron exclaimed, "That's the cat that was on the flyers in our neighborhood!" I recalled seeing "lost cat" flyers posted on street signs, but this cat didn't resemble that one.

"Aaron," I said. "I don't think this is the same cat. Besides, even if it is, those flyers were posted several months ago. They've long since come down."

As we walked back through our neighborhood, Aaron scanned every piece of litter he saw. I was incredulous when he yelled, "Here's one!" Sure enough, in the middle of a yard Aaron had found a two-inch strip of what had once been the full-sized sheet. After several months out in the weather, the paper was very worn and tattered. The amazing part was that the tiny scrap that remained included the owner's phone number. Aaron urged me to call the number. I was afraid of giving this person false hope since I was convinced this wasn't their cat and, even if it was, the poor thing was at death's door.

At Aaron's insistence, I called. The young lady who answered, Sarah, verified that she lost a cat about three months earlier. They had moved to neighboring apartments and the first day there the cat, an indoor pet not used to being outside, accidentally got out. Although she was overjoyed that I had called, I quickly explained the situation to her and cautioned her that I wasn't even sure if it was her cat and that, if it was, it was very sick.

Within ten minutes, she was at our house, but when we drove to the place where the cat was last seen, it was nowhere to be found. This poor creature could barely take a step. Where could it have gone? As we walked around the area, she started calling its name.

"Gracie, he-e-ere Gracie," she called.

We heard a very faint "meow." We all stood still to listen.

"Gracie, here Gracie."

Once again, a very faint meow was heard coming from...ten feet below in the sewer under the street. The poor cat had apparently staggered sideways into the storm drain. Sarah frantically got down on her hands and knees and looked through the hole in the manhole cover. Sure enough, it was her missing cat, Gracie! Poor Gracie had obviously sustained several other injuries during the fall. She was bleeding from a large abrasion on her forehead and her jaw appeared to be broken and horribly out of alignment. She lay on her side unable to even lift her head. "Terrific," I thought. "We brought this poor girl here only to watch her cat die in the sewer."

After we pulled off the manhole cover, Sarah started to climb into the sewer. Fearing for her safety, Dan stopped her and convinced her to wait for animal control to help. Within minutes, a man from animal control appeared on the scene, took one look at Gracie and shook his head. Although he would retrieve her, he didn't hold out much hope for her survival. A moment later, Mr. Animal Control was placing a completely unresponsive Gracie into the loving arms of her owner. Sarah was adamant about giving Aaron a $40 reward. Dan flatly refused, saying that we couldn't possibly take her money. I saw the excitement fade from Aaron's face, so I agreed when Sarah insisted on at least giving him $20. Sarah thanked us profusely and whisked Gracie away, headed for the vet's office. Mr. Animal Control made the grim pronouncement that he feared Sarah would spend more money to have the vet put Gracie to sleep.

I didn't hear from Sarah for several days and was sure little Gracie had passed away. I waited about a week and curiosity got the better of me, so I called Sarah. After a few niceties, I asked about Gracie.

"Gracie? Oh, she's doing great!" came her chipper reply.

"What? Great?" I asked, startled. I'd expected the word 'dead', not 'great.'

"The vet said that it was simply severe malnutrition and dehydration that made her look that way and stagger like that. He told me to go home and give her plenty of food and water, and she would be fine."

"What about the abrasion on her head and the broken jaw?" I asked.

"Oh, her head is healing nicely and her jaw was just dislocated. The vet told me to give her dry, crunchy cat food and the chewing would pop the jaw back into place. I tried it, and sure enough, while she was trying to eat, her jaw popped back into place. Thank you again so much for giving me the best Christmas ever!" Sarah gushed.

As I hung up the phone, I could hardly believe what I'd heard. Talk about nine lives! Gracie had to be the luckiest cat on earth. In her weakened condition, there is no way she could have escaped from that drainage sewer. She would have died down there out of sight of any help. The area in which she fell had no nearby homes so even if she cried out, it is doubtful anyone would have heard her. What was the likelihood that we happened to see her moments before her fateful fall,

Aaron happened to recognize her, and we happened to find a tiny scrap of paper with her owner's number on it? It's at times like these that I am convinced God uses His creation as a model to demonstrate His intricate spiritual principles.

I've often thought of the helplessness of that cat and her utter dependence on God's intervention when I think of my own need for a Savior. I was that cat, helpless and lying in the gutter with no hope of ever rescuing myself. However, just as Gracie was saved in the nick of time, so God saved helpless me.

> "But God, being rich in mercy, because of the great love with which He loved us, even when we were dead in our trespasses, made us alive together with Christ – by grace you have been saved – and raised us up with Him and seated us with Him in the heavenly places in Christ Jesus, so that in the coming ages He might show the immeasurable riches of His grace in kindness toward us in Christ Jesus. For by grace you have been saved through faith; and that not of yourselves, it is the gift of God; not a result of works, so that no one may boast." (Ephesians 2:4-8)

CHAPTER 26

The Gift of a New House

MARCH 2016 FOUND us living in our original home in Aiken, where we had been for the past 31 years. For several months we felt the need to complete kitchen renovations, but we had our reservations about whether or not we would ever recoup the investment. After much prayer, we dipped our toe into the idea of moving to a newer home that would require less care. We were doubtful that we would sell our home easily, since it was not in one of the more desirable neighborhoods, it didn't have the popular open floor plan people seemed to want, and the local housing market had been sluggish for a long time.

On March 6, 2016 we looked online and picked out a few suitable homes. When we drove around to look at those homes, we were surprised to find that five of the seven we had chosen already were under contract. We took this to mean that the housing market was more brisk than we thought and that we might be able to sell our house in a timely manner after all. On March 10 we contacted a realtor. We set to work on the items she delineated that would need to be taken care of before we listed our current home for sale. Most of these items were relatively minor and were swiftly accomplished.

On March 17 our realtor showed us our first three homes. We made the decision to try to sell our home and listed it with the agent on March 23, 2017. The morning was spent with the agency taking photographs of our home and bringing a "For Sale" sign to place in front of our house. The realtor commented that it would possibly take until 4:00 p.m. that afternoon for our listing to first show up on the area realtors' web sites as well as on Zillow, an online tool for buying and selling homes. At 5:30 that evening before we were even aware that our listing was complete, I received a phone call from a third party realtor.

"How would you like to sell your home today?" she asked.

I laughed. "Sure, that would be great," I kidded.

She told me that in her office was a couple who had been looking for a home for a while, and the three of them had planned to visit several more homes that evening.

"Your house just popped up as a new listing today. They've looked at the specifications and photos, and they are pretty darn excited. Can I bring them over in an hour?" she asked.

"Sure. It's clean as a whistle since we just took photos today," I quipped.

Sure enough, she and her clients walked through our house at 6:30, and at 7:30 we received a call from the realtor telling us to expect a formal contract the next day. True to their word, we received a formal contract on our home the next day, March 24th. It had been on the market for a total of one hour.

On March 26 we signed a contract to buy a house on Granger Street in South Meadows, our desired neighborhood. Although I was only mildly enthusiastic about this house, I agreed to it because Dan was so excited about it. I reasoned that in anything in life, it was quite normal for one partner in a marriage to be more excited than the other in any given decision. I was quite sure I would begin to feel more enthusiastic about that decision. Much to my surprise, as time went on I only felt worse. My reservations about the Granger house grew, but I was determined to let the Lord either change my feelings or, if not, to let Him change Dan's mind.

On April 24th I attended a Fierce Women retreat in Hilton Head with several of my friends. When we were each given the opportunity to tell the group the main challenge we would be facing upon returning home, I shared my concerns with these ladies and asked them to pray for God's grace in my life to do His will regarding the house even though I didn't really want to buy the Granger house. The next day, April 25th, without a word from me, Dan came to the conclusion that we should get out of that contract. Some problems with the flooring that couldn't be resolved in that house became apparent that day. I was shocked to hear my husband approach me and declare that we needed to break the contract.

The next day was the last day we could get our earnest money back so we had to move quickly. I started to question his decision to make sure he was certain, but told myself to be quiet because this was exactly the miracle I had hoped for. However, I also knew that my husband didn't want to move twice and the May closing date on our current home was fast approaching. I thanked the Lord for showing Dan the wisdom of getting out of the contract on the Granger house and told Him I trusted Him to show us which house he had in mind. I also reminded Him that the decision needed to be made the next day so it would be great if He could please show me the way that evening.

I should mention that Dan and I had a tongue-in-cheek joke just between the two of us that the address of any home God would give us would necessarily be either 31 or 131 because all the homes we ever owned up to that point contained those numbers. Several interesting facts dawned on us during this process that we had never before considered. The closing date the bank set for our current house was May 31, 2016, the exact same day we had closed on it 31 years prior. I realized I was 31 years old when we bought that house, and we had lived in it for exactly 31 years.

Although we had already exhausted our search in several neighborhoods and I knew there were no other homes on the market in our price range that we hadn't previously discounted, I looked on Zillow once more. This time I expanded my search by letting the cursor sweep over homes for sale in a part of the neighborhood that was even more desirable than we had been looking at, but was out of our price range. When I looked at a home for sale in this choice part of the subdivision, it was $5,000 over our price range, but I also noted it was a foreclosure, which I knew could be acquired for a good deal less than the asking price. The photos were not well done and it was difficult to get a good feel for the house. But the basic facts were what we wanted, so I forwarded the listing to Dan's email and moved on with my evening activities. I was actually grocery shopping when Dan called.

"That house you sent me looks pretty good, and can you believe the address?"

"I never noticed the address. What is it?" I asked.

"131," he answered, much to my amusement.

Nothing is coincidental with God. You already know the rest of the story. That, my friends, is the fabulous house the Lord gave us. Dan and I both agree it is much nicer than anything we had ever looked at or even hoped to have. Although it was a foreclosure, it was in excellent condition. We were released from our contract on the Granger house on April 26th and put an offer on the 131 house that same day. The bank agreed to an asking price that was within our original price range. We closed on our new home on June 9, 2016, resting assured that it was definitely a gift from God.

CHAPTER 27

Grandparenting: A Crazy Kind of Love

"May you live to see your children's children."
~ Psalm 128:6

WHEN ASHLEY WAS pregnant with my first grandchild, I had fellow grandparents constantly telling me how thrilling it was to become a grandparent. Ashley was with me when one woman, commenting on a grandparent's love for her grandchildren, said, "It's a crazy kind of love!" I don't recall who it was that said that to me, but I have to say she was right on the money. Witnessing Margo being born and taking her first breath was one of the most stunning moments of my life! The love I've experienced since becoming a grandmother is "a crazy kind of love." Margo, Riley, JD, Andrew, and Landon have been by far some of the greatest sources of pure rapture I have ever experienced. The pleasure of enjoying grandchildren is a good example of God saving the best for last.

In a prophetic statement foretelling the birth of Christ through David's line, God blesses David's house and promises to establish His eternal kingdom on it. In 2 Samuel 7:18, King David says to God "Who am I, O Lord? And what is my house, that you have brought me this far?" David was a sinful man and he knew it, and he was humbled by God's promises to him. Verses like these compel me to ask God to bless my descendants forever. Is anything too hard for Him? I've asked God that every grandchild or grandchildren yet to be born and all future descendants until He returns would have new life in Christ. Scripture says we have not because we ask not, so I come boldly before Him and ask. That means if you are one of my descendants, I have already prayed that God would open your eyes of understanding to see that Jesus is the one true God through Whom we have eternal life. "And there is salvation in no one else, for there is no other name under heaven given among men by which we must be saved." (Acts 4:12) What could make heaven more perfect than to live eternally with an awesome God full of love? Well, nothing is truly going to top that, but the desire of my heart is that heaven will also be filled with every descendant of mine until He returns.

If I were writing the script, I would have all my children and grandchildren live very close by. But they do not. Ashley and her family's recent move to the West Coast has been a significant challenge for me, but it has also been an opportunity for me to either grumble and complain or to get on board with what God is doing. When I am faced with accepting the unwanted in my life, I have found it helpful to give myself the freedom to acknowledge the loss and feelings of disappointment. This seems to make room for me to release that expectation and eagerly embrace God's change of plans and His will for me. As I submit to His new plans, I often have to ask Him to "show me how to do this." He has never let me down, and I have faith that carries me through each new situation.

And so I have come full circle. I stated in the beginning that describing God's faithfulness to my children and grandchildren has been the great motivation that has propelled me to write this. My children and grandchildren are my greatest inspiration. What a privilege that I have been given the gift of life long enough to see another generation.

During the times when I am most enraptured by the love I give to and get from my grandkids, I find it awesome to think that heaven will be even better than that. "Your love is better than life." (Psalm 63:3) Imagine that! Just take a minute to truly imagine what that is saying. Experiencing the fullness of God's love is better than any joy we can experience in life. Imagine a love that is greater than that exhilaration of having a baby, greater than the blissful feeling of falling in love. Better than any amazing sights we have seen, foods we have eaten, friends we have enjoyed, grandchildren we have loved, fun we have had. All those experiences combined will pale in comparison to experiencing God's love. And we will experience it for all eternity. Wow!

One thing I have desired of the Lord,
That will I seek:
That I may dwell in the house of the Lord
All the days of my life,
To behold the beauty of the Lord,
And to inquire in His temple.

For in the time of trouble
He shall hide me in His pavilion;
In the secret place of His tabernacle
He shall hide me;
He shall set me high upon a rock.

Psalm 27:4-5

CHAPTER 28

Finishing Strong

*"So even to old age and gray hairs, O God, do not forsake me,
until I proclaim Your might to another generation,
Your power to all those to come."*
~ Psalm 71:18

"He will renew your life and sustain you in your old age."
~ Ruth 4:15

I FIND MYSELF spending more and more time quieting my soul in the Lord. In our materialistic society, it's easy to be discontented and feel like I need more and more. Our American culture breeds excess. It's very difficult to be moderate in our food choices and material goods. A saying I heard recently captures it well: "Why complain that the roses have thorns when you can celebrate that the thorns have roses?"

According to C.S. Lewis, "You are never too old to set another goal or dream another dream." However, after retirement, I experienced a sense of finality and even a sense of loss about my future. I also struggled with my focus. I wrestled with trying to be content where God had put me. We all have to choose what direction we will face. Will we strive after bigger, better, or more exciting exploits? We are called to be good stewards of the bodies God has given us, yet to be content with the health that we have and the circumstances of our lives. As I pondered these things, I studied Luke 12. I confessed discontent and worry as sin, and I asked God to help me to be content with my location, my financial status, my future, and my health.

One day I noticed the petunia planters on my front porch. I wanted to turn the planters around since the back of the pot was prettier than the front and I wanted the beautiful part to face the street. I turned the planters around, knowing that the plants would eventually grow toward the front of the pot because that was the direction of the sun. I noticed the next day that nothing much had changed about the plants. The following day the plants seemed to be turning just a little bit in the other direction. I forgot about the flowers, and a week later I was sitting on my front porch reading and praying through Luke 12, asking God to show me what He wanted for the focus of my life. The verses I was reading began with "consider the lilies." I lifted my head to ponder what I'd just read, and it was then that I noticed those petunias.

Imperceptibly, over many days, those little blossoms had completely changed direction. They were now facing out towards the sun, and they had never looked prettier. The focus of their lives had completely changed. They knew where their life source was. I couldn't make those living creatures turn, but their Creator could. Every little head was turned toward the sunshine. They were not just content, they were flourishing. They had turned their little backs on the house, people, and everything else that was less important than their Sustainer. God reminded me that that is what He wants for my life. I need to lean into the "Sonshine." He doesn't care where the rest of the world is looking. He wants my focus to be imperceptibly, year after year, turned toward Him.

If my focus is where it should be, toward the Creator and Sustainer of my life, it might look very different from many other people in this world. Remaining content will have its own sense of beauty, because I will be fulfilled in Him. Just like the petunias, the face of my life will be stretched out, with my chin up, and my eyes looking up for His strengthening, His sustaining power, and His nourishment. That will be my good pleasure, "looking unto Him, the Author and Finisher of [my] faith." (Hebrews 12:2) I thanked those little petunias for showing me how beautiful it can be to completely rely on your Creator, and I asked God to help me to be half as pliable as they were.

Jesus is not only God Himself, but also the quintessentially thankful human. The God-man not only died to forgive our failures, He also lived the perfect life of appreciation on our behalf toward His Father. And so the apostle Paul encourages Christians to have lives characterized by thanksgiving. "As you received Christ Jesus the Lord, so walk in him, rooted and built up in him and established in the faith, just as you were taught, abounding in thanksgiving." (Colossians 2:6-7)

It is fitting for a creature to be in a continuous posture of gratitude toward his Creator. And it is even more fitting for a redeemed rebel to be in an ongoing posture of gratitude toward his Redeemer. I am that rebel, living the kind of life that flows from such amazing grace that I aspire to live a life of continual thankfulness. I yearn to be continually renewed, progressively being made more like Jesus, and always thankful.

According to John Piper, my life is not like the setting of the sun at the end of the day, it is like the ever growing brightness of the rising sun. "The path of the righteous is like the light of dawn, shining brighter and brighter until midday." (Proverbs 4:18) So the aim of my life is to shine brighter, live richer and reflect more fully the beautiful grace of the True Light that is coming at full noon.

In many ways, now is the best time of my life. I really do believe God saved the best for last. At 64 years of age, I am happier than I've ever been in my life. Let's face it; retirement, grandparenting, freedom to minister and to travel – those are pretty glorious gifts. On the other hand, in all reality, the next truly big event in my future is going home to glory. I didn't say dying because I am not planning to die. I will never see death. "Truly, truly, I say to you, if anyone keeps my word, he will never see death." (John 8:51) Sons of God do not die, they are glorified. Humanity is enslaved globally to a pervasive, life-long fear of death. It haunts the human animal. It is a fear which is rarely spoken of, but one which never goes unfelt. We find all kinds of ways to deny and numb this fear. However, Jesus' victory over death and the liberating truths of Hebrews 2:14 have allowed me to live a life free of the fear of death and to embrace a life of adventure and risk. It also allows me to fearlessly embrace the future.

> "Since therefore the children share in flesh and blood [we are human], He himself likewise partook of the same nature [He became human] so that through death He might destroy the one who has the power of death, that is the devil, and deliver all those who through the fear of death were subject to lifelong slavery."
> (Hebrews 2:14)

Romans 8:16-17 says "The Spirit Himself bears witness with our spirit that we are children of God and if children, then heirs – heirs of God and fellow heirs with Christ, provided we suffer with Him in order that we may also be glorified with Him." It's not the being glorified part that worries me. It's the suffering part. Everyone wants to reach a ripe old age and die painlessly in their sleep. No one chooses pain, but if it's God's will for me to suffer, then I want to be a faithful sufferer.

As I look toward the end of my life, I lean on these words from Martin Luther: "I have held many things in my hands, and I have lost them all; but whatever I have placed in God's hands, that I still possess." I hope to face the future with an ever-present sense of hope. This hope is based on what I've learned: that even in difficult seasons of suffering and loss, I can and do experience joy because the joy comes from communing with the Lord, not necessarily from my circumstances. I also know the Lord is always calling us to a greater walk, not necessarily a greater work. When we formally retire from earning a living, it's easy to feel as though we are being put out to pasture. Lord willing, I still have many productive years ahead of me, and I plan to wear out for the Lord rather than rust out. Regardless of my past or future accomplishments, I remember that my value is based on my identity in Christ and that being included in God's family is the highest honor and the greatest privilege I will ever receive. Nothing else comes close. Whenever I feel unimportant, unloved or insecure, I remember to Whom I belong. Jesus has called me into relationship with Him, and because of what Christ has done, "I have now met the standard of the only One in the universe whose opinion of me matters." (John Franks, New Covenant Presbyterian Church)

When all is said and done, George Herbert's poem, "Secretary of Praise," inspires me as he points out that my job on this planet, and yours, is that we are secretaries of the praise of our awesome God.

Secretary of Praise
by George Herbert

Of all the creatures both in sea and land
Only to man thou hast made known Thy ways,
And put the pen alone into his hand,
And made him secretary of Thy praise.

I may lack eloquence, but my desire is to awaken praise of God. That is what language is for. If this book will move one person to praise God even once because of the words in it, then writing it will have been time well spent. In Hosea 12:10, God himself says He inspires writers to use words to touch men's hearts: "I spoke to the prophets; it was I who multiplied visions, and through the prophets gave parables."

If we let God write our story, He doesn't promise that all the chapters will be easy, but He does promise that in the last chapter He will make sense of them, terribly painful though they may have been. I close with this little poem, which encourages me greatly and reminds me that the knowledge of God will always be the supreme source of joy in any life.

I Stood A Mendicant [Beggar]
by Martha Snell Nicholson

I stood a mendicant of God before His royal throne
And begged of Him for one priceless gift, which I could call my own.
I took the gift from out His hand, but as I would depart
I cried, "But Lord this is a thorn and it has pierced my heart.
This is a strange, a hurtful gift, which Thou hast given me."
He said, "My child, I give good gifts and gave My best to thee."
I took it home and though at first the cruel thorn hurt sore,
As long years passed I learned at last to love it more and more.
I learned He never gives a thorn without this added grace,
He takes the thorn to pin aside the veil which hides His face.

ABOUT THE AUTHOR

Peggy Margo Wojtowicz is a wife, mother of two, grandmother of five, and a retired medical assistant who struggled with paralyzing anxieties until she experienced the hand of God in her life. You can contact her at peggywojo@gmail.com or find her on Facebook as Peggy Margo Wojtowicz.